THE
WHOLE
TRUTH
ABOUT
SPIRULINA

Documented results by users and health care professionals

Introduction by Dr. Christopher Hills

Foreword by Dr. Lendon H. Smith

Edited by Wendy Fulcher

NEW ERA PRESS
Scottsdale, Arizona

THE WHOLE TRUTH ABOUT SPIRULINA

Printed in United States of America by Banta Company.

Library of Congress Cataloging in Publication Data

Main entry under title:

The Whole truth about Spirulina.

    1. Spirulina—Therapeutic use—Miscellanea.
I. Fulcher, Wendy, 1948–
RM666.S663W48   1982   613.2'8   82–24518
ISBN 0–9610380–0–4

Contents

Introduction
by Christopher Hills, Ph.D., D.Sc.

After twenty years of research into different kinds of edible microalgae, looking for a safe and nutritious food, we found the superfood Spirulina. Without the disadvantages of Anabaena and other algaes which can become toxic, Spirulina has been proved to be safe to eat for hundreds of years in those countries where it grows naturally. The fact that Spirulina's remarkable properties have been investigated by United Nations agencies and researched by French, German and Japanese nutritionists, medical doctors and microbiologists of worldwide fame has not stopped a few academicians from trying to smear Spirulina's name and to minimize its fantastic results.

This book is a direct positive answer to those few negative "experts" who have been carrying on their own campaign, saying Spirulina is some kind of fad or is nutritionally deficient. Over and over we see that the results speak for themselves. As yet, there has been no American research into the therapeutic aspects of Spirulina but this book offers firsthand reports from people who have actually used it. There is a good reason why there is no medical research into Spirulina in this country. Such research would not be acceptable to the FDA because according to those authorities any research showing medical effects would automatically turn Spirulina from a food into a drug. This strange attitude is the particular mind-set of a group of bureaucrats who think they know better. Since they have power that no ordinary citizen has, they are allowed to dictate what should be said about a product.

Of course, in America, every citizen has the power of free speech. So it was with great delight that I greeted Wendy Fulcher's proposal to publish a book on the benefits of Spirulina. Thank God we live in a free society where individual freedom to publish one's ideas has not been taken away. However, were this book to be used to sell Spirulina, one's constitutional rights would be negated by the FDA's power over what one can say about a product one distributes.

The ideals of free thinking and free enterprise were part of the pioneering spirit that built this nation. Yet today we see a society whose creativity is crippled by a huge government bureaucracy which kills all incentive to do business or create anything new. I have personally had to pay dearly for my commitment to seeing Spirulina made available in a hungry world. A food whose potential is unlimited, has been stopped nearly every step along its arduous path by excessive government regulation and red tape. Because I hold this belief so firmly and passionately that the fifteen million bureaucrats have killed the individual pioneering spirit of America, I am hoping the publication of these unsolicited letters will acquaint people with the truth about Spirulina. And I hope you will write to the publisher with your own experiences and stand up for the truth you believe in! Only through individual citizens' personal experience and truth-seekers speaking out will we ever counteract the negativity and "wet blanket" of bureaucracy.

While I agree that the public should have some protection from charlatans and "snake oil" salesmen who foist false products upon them, I observe these same authorities approving drugs which, upon deeper investigation, have disastrous effects upon people, e.g., thalido-mide, cyclamates, valium, and others whose real effects are only now being discovered by millions of unwitting human guinea pigs. These same authorities do nothing to act against dozens of the mislabelled or phoney Spirulina products that appeared on the market during late 1981. What a system we live with!

Here in this book is a cross section of letters actually received which I never asked for. There must be thousands who used Spirulina who never thought of writing letters and hundreds more who thought of writing but who never did do it. (A great pity.)

Here are a few of the ones who did. Their everyday experience must speak for itself.

I am grateful to Wendy Fulcher and to New Era Press for the courage to publish this book against the conspiracy of people who would suffocate the information these letters contain and suppress it in the name of "the people."

I believe those government servants and experts who claim superior knowledge and appear to work for the benefit and protection of the people are in fact their worst enemy when it comes to the introduction of new products and new information.

I hope you stand up for your rights too. Don't let the bureaucrats run your life; eat Spirulina.

Yours in truth,

Christopher Hills

Foreword
by Dr. Lendon H. Smith

Spirulina is an efficient, relatively inexpensive method of getting proper minerals into the human system. With the known decrease of minerals in our topsoil most people find they need supplements to maintain health. The minerals incorporated in Spirulina are easily absorbed through the intestinal tract wall. The vitamins and proteins that are incorporated in Spirulina make all these things work in a normal physiological way.

Dr. Lendon Smith, America's foremost pediatrician, is known nationwide through his best-selling books *Feed Your Kids Right*, and *Foods for Healthy Kids* and his television appearances as "The Children's Doctor." The central message of his work is clear: poor nutrition is often the real cause of health and behavior difficulties in children, and this can be prevented by proper eating. Dr. Smith shows in case after case, when the natural biochemistry of these children is restored with right eating, that their whole world changes from the inside out, and they become happy and healthy, and vibrant with life. Dr. Smith naturally appreciates the role Spirulina can play in an excellent nutritional program to safeguard the health of both children and adults.

Editor's Foreword

I first became acquainted with Spirulina about three years ago through a friend in the office where I worked. She was on a "Spirulina fast"—blending up the Spirulina powder with apple juice, bananas, and frozen strawberries. It made a delicious concoction and my friend had never looked better. She was beaming. I started taking Spirulina on a daily basis soon after that and found I no longer had the 10:00 a.m. energy slump at work that usually sent me after a cup of tea or coffee. I couldn't believe it. On my first fast I felt wonderful sensations of energy in my body as if my internal organs were being bathed in some form of life-giving essence. As time went by, Spirulina and I became fast friends. I read about Spirulina, its incredible nutritional make-up and the research that was being done to make this food available to the poor and hungry of the world. And I began hearing all kinds of wonderful stories of people who'd had experiences like my own, and far more amazing ones. What better way to share the Spirulina news with others, I thought, than through a collection of these personal, heart-warming accounts—perhaps letters—from people whose lives were changing because of Spirulina.

Spirulina is not a drug; it is a wonderful food. As such Spirulina is meant to supplement the user's health program, and not to replace any drugs prescribed by the physician. It is left to you, the reader, to try Spirulina and discover for yourself its benefits.

I want to thank Dr. Christopher Hills, author of several books on Spirulina and a real pioneer in making Spirulina known and available to the American public, for his help in making this project possible. He was the recipient of most of the letters in this book, which came to him unsolicited, and he kindly turned them over to me for the book. In addition, I contacted several health care professionals, including doctors, chiropractors, nurses, and nutritionists who have their own perspective on Spirulina. Their letters are included here in Chapter 12. I would also like to extend my thanks to New Era Press, which, with the publication of this book, contributes to a new era of nutritional abundance for all of mankind.

Note: This book does not constitute an endorsement of any specific brand or product, but is merely a report of the benefits of Spirulina as reported by consumers and health care professionals. Bracketed and/or asterisked material throughout the book indicates that actual product names have been withheld due to FDA regulations.

Wendy Fulcher

Chapter 1

FOOD AND FOOD SUPPLEMENT

2

Spirulina, a safe, natural vegetable food, has been called by many a miracle of nutrition. The reasons are simple. Spirulina contains most of the vitamins and minerals your body needs, all of the essential protein-building amino acids, and in addition trace elements, cell salts, and enzymes required by the human system. In fact, nature blessed this little vegetable organism with such an abundance of nutrients in well-balanced distribution for the human system that a Japanese philosopher has been able to live on Spirulina alone for years, demonstrating to everyone that there is an answer to the world's hunger problem—a simple blue-green plankton that grows in light and water—Spirulina. But the miracle doesn't end with Spirulina's nutritional profile. Even more unusual is the way Spirulina makes its nutrients available to your body. The proteins are in forms you could almost call predigested—in fact they are on the average 90% digestible as compared to meat's 20%. In addition, its rare carbohydrates and vitamins and minerals are also easily absorbed—they come to your body just as Mother Nature made them. No wonder people are calling Spirulina the staple of the future, the health food of today.

Excellent source of natural nutrition

After teaching school for twenty-two years in one of the worst ghettos imaginable, I took an early retirement because of the stress and strain. And because of Spirulina, I believe I will live to enjoy many more years. I have been a regular user for many months now. I am positive that Spirulina is the most excellent source of natural nutrition ever made available for human consumption. Almost daily I persuade my friends to use it as a food.

San Antonio, TX

I was skeptical, at first, about Spirulina; but after trying a fast and using Spirulina for the past month and a half, I am no longer. I feel more energy, mental and physical; and I feel better about myself than I've felt for a long time. I am excited about turning people on to this amazing superfood.

I would like to put together a portfolio of Spirulina Nutritional Information to hand out to doctors and nutritionists, chiropractors, and others in the health-related fields in my area, in hopes that they will start experimenting with Spirulina on their clients and start using this wonderfood themselves. I am convinced that vitamins and minerals do not stand up to this natural substance.

Athens, OH

The recent research on the potential of plankton algae to be an incredible nutritional source of rapidly assimilated food has led me to Spirulina. Recently, a colleague of mine told me of his experience in using Spirulina, saying that it is an amazing source of energy. As a researcher of medical nutrition it has been my bottom line experience that those supplements that have the greatest assimilation power are the true super foods and should be marketed as the real "Vitamins."

Santa Monica, CA

My husband and I have been very pleased with Spirulina and had it almost every day for the last year for breakfast in orange juice. We find it more satisfying than a regular bacon and egg breakfast.

We fasted on Spirulina and juices for several weeks and felt increased vigor, no hunger pangs and much less need for sleep. We lost about a pound a day!

Zephyr Cove, NV

"Spirulina is my 'meat' and staple."

Since December, 1980, I have been eating Spirulina, diluted in water, every day and it is what I have based my diet on. I eat supplemental portions of starches and vegetables and fruits, etc., but on the whole Spirulina is my "meat" and staple. I am a very poor music student and this has been a very economical diet, to say the least! The two most salient features of this kind of nutrition on me are my fingernails which are now absolutely beautiful and long and white and strong, and my hair, which has been very thin, appears now thicker with wonderful sheen and less split ends. These are really noticeable. Also, I haven't been very sick this year . . . maybe once I got down and suffered a throat ache. Also my muscle tone has improved . . . my physical shape looks better. And I know very well that it gives me energy. On an empty stomach, somewhat tired, I take a level tablespoon of Spirulina and do a 2 hour exercise-workout with ease. I am very grateful to have the knowledge of Spirulina in my life!

Burbank, CA

I have recently become acquainted with Spirulina and have quickly learned to appreciate some of its qualities. The work I do is extremely arduous physical labor and for years I have relied upon nutritional yeast to give me the endurance to work all day. Spirulina with chlorophyll rounds out my diet very well since I often don't take the time to cook greens with my meal.

Trout Creek, MT

After having consumed some 4–5 pounds [of Spirulina] so far, I do not see how I can possibly live without it and wonder how I managed to live to the age of 47 as well as I have.

To begin with -- I had a tremendous loss of energy at about the age of 28 – I was tired all the time in spite of hours and hours of sleep. So, I became my own guinea pig -- spent fortunes on books on health and at health food stores trying to achieve a vibrant state of good health. Still about all I managed to do was to exist and keep away from Doctors' offices and hospitals.

Approximately 6 months ago I "discovered" Spirulina. Prior to this I had been on a cleansing program along with a whole raw foods diet. This was great up to a point -- the point where I reached a severe protein shortage. While I was nice and slim (incidentally I never was fat – 5'6" and always maintained a weight of 120–130 lbs.), I was very flabby, my body did not seem to have any substance to it. I find of course that exercise will firm up your muscles to a point -- but you have to keep on exercising. With the Spirulina I find a beautiful firmness and have not been exercising. I pass this information on to you as there may be other people like myself who work at a desk job and cannot get the time to exercise as we should. My own particular circumstances are such that exercise is difficult in the winter months. I live on an acreage 16½ miles from work. I get up at 6 in the morning – get ready for work – drive to town – sit at my desk from 8 till 5 – drive home – prepare supper, etc. It is always dark when I leave for work and dark when I get home. The weather is about 30–40° below zero from January to March. So Spirulina is great for keeping a nice firm healthy body – when you find yourself in such circumstances where you cannot exercise – or other similar situations if one is bedridden, crippled or recovering from a bad accident that may require a lengthy stay in bed or a wheelchair.

Thanks to Spirulina I can now quit being a guinea pig and having to experiment with so many various brands of vitamins and minerals. Spirulina is all I need. I really enjoy its flavor – and have become a bit greedy in that I like to eat it 3 or 4 times a day.

Lloydminster, Alberta

Solar energy for mothers

I would like to share an uplifting personal experience that I recently had, with hopes that it may help some others who at this time are seeking an answer to their low physical energy dilemma.

It was a difficult reality for me to accept at first but I had to ask myself, "Are some mothers starving while nursing their children?" I think this could be very possible. As we all know, we need increased nutrients during lactation. Whether or not we are receiving complete nutrients will depend upon how our body metabolizes the foods we eat and the *quality* of the food we eat. This is questionable in our culture today even if one is preparing foods in proper combinations or buying foods from co-op or health food stores.

Since my first child, I did not have all the understanding of the changes each stage of mothering brings. Although my pregnancy was strong and vibrant, I was not prepared for what followed during nursing and actual mothering. Sleep, diet, and emotions were all out of sync for quite a long time after the birth. It felt like I had danced a long waltz for nine months that was followed by a polka which I never quite caught all the steps for.

I finally started to get the hint that exhaustion and occasional depression which I experienced coincided with the amount of sleep I received, but still the hardest thing to grasp was diet. I couldn't believe that my dedicated whole foods combining wasn't nutritionally sufficient to sustain me and [my child]. Along with some refined advice on food combining came the suggested addition of the food that dramatically changed my life at this stage. This addition was Spirulina plankton.

After using Spirulina for only 1 week, I regained complete energy and vitality as I had once remembered it long before my first child. My milk supply also increased in that first week and has maintained itself since. I began to have a strong belief that many mothers are dragging their heels in the streets literally starved for proper nutrition.

Spirulina is captured sunlight through photosynthesis. Mothers (and fathers) deserve the highest quality food, food from sunlight. If this little bit of information can help any parent I will be very happy.

Stillwater, MN

From a wife and mother

What a remarkable food substance Spirulina plankton is! And the possibilities for its use in the future are encouraging.

Right now I am very interested in it for myself, my husband and two small boys, ages 4 and 1. I was amazed to learn what a complete and nutritious food it is and am anxious to experiment with it by incorporating it into our daily diets. I do enjoy to fast every now and then and soon will start my yearly birthday fast for at least 2 weeks.

Truckee, CA

Mixed with tomato juice it [Spirulina] completely satisfies my hunger. My energy level does not seem to suffer when I am fasting with Spirulina; in fact, mixed with tomato juice and cayenne pepper, it gives me an energy buzz for about an hour.

Boulder Creek, CA

We feel so much better since we have been taking Spirulina. It is a marvelous food.

Ash Flat, AR

I have been enjoying the benefits of Spirulina for about 6 months now and have introduced many of my friends and co-workers to this wonderful food.

Cambridge, MA

Spirulina—a survival food

I have been taking it [Spirulina] for one month now and I am completely sold on it as a survival food. It's great for losing weight naturally too!

Pacific Grove, CA

In my holistic practice I have always been searching for new superfoods and found Spirulina to be among the best, for which reason I often recommended it to others.

Staten Island, NY

Five years of personal experimentation of a total non-animal diet (introducing Spirulina two years ago), has brought me to believe that Spirulina is one of the most powerful foods on earth (including wheatgrass).

Eureka, CA

Ever since 1975 I have been searching for a certain food, not knowing what it was, that would be complete and that would enable me to fast. Finally this year I have found it in Spirulina and am very thankful. At this point I am consuming one bottle of 200 Spirulina tablets each week.

Cambridge, MA

Spirulina is the most perfect food I have ever experienced. It's truly *wonderful*! Perhaps even the immediate precursor to Soma? I've found if I combine 1 Tbsp. of Spirulina with a big bowl of Bieler's Broth (Bieler's was my favorite food before Spirulina announced itself. It's equal parts fresh green beans, celery, zucchini, lightly steamed and then homogenized with a bunch of fresh parsley) 4–6 times a day; it's the only food I need to keep me happy, lively and effective in whatever activity I'm engaged in.

San Diego, CA

I have now been using [X brand] for several months and find it a superlative nutrient. Of course I go on eating what I have been eating but am no longer hungry. Having been a vegetarian for 20 years and a Vegan for 10, this form of protein is a nutrient this body accepts with relief and joy.

Carmel Valley, CA

I very much like the effects Spirulina has on my body (much better than wheat grass), and its potential efficiency for feeding many people in the world ecologically.

Arvada, CO

Food of the future

We have been using Spirulina for some time and feel it is a remarkable product. And in my opinion, it could easily become the food of the future.

Warrenton, MO

I will be leaving in approximately two weeks or earlier. I am especially interested in helping the Tibetan refugees in India and Cambodian refugees in Thailand. If you wish I will distribute Spirulina to the needy.

New Hyde Park, NY

P.S. I myself have fasted for five weeks on juices, herbs and Spirulina, and am well aware of its great potential and efficacy.

Managing "hidden hunger"

I've been experimenting with Spirulina with great interest ever since being introduced to it by a friend about a year ago. I've been a health practitioner and student of nutrition for years, but no single food has ever had such a dramatic effect on my systems as did the [X brand]. Not only did I notice an immediate metabolic change and a new ability to manage "hidden hunger", but my energy level expressed spiritually and intellectually seemed to take a quantum leap, although many factors besides [Spirulina] have aided in that transformation.

Hope, ID

Would like to tell you what Spirulina has done for us. My husband has lost 25 lbs. in 2 months and I have lost 11 lbs., and we have cut our grocery bill by 50%. We have lost our desire for red meat. We eat salads, vegetables, seafood and chicken. We feel better, have more energy, and I have had no problems with my 3 ulcers! and no pain! We are born again in good health and feel terrific!

Dunwoody, GA

I've been into nutrition twenty years searching for the perfect diet -- not until Spirulina came along did I experience it!

No. Hollywood, CA

After using Spirulina plankton as a diet supplement and major protein source, I am convinced that Spirulina is the most important food on the planet. I hope that you can supply me with sufficient quantities to use it for myself, and to turn my friends on to its life supporting qualities.

Arvada, CO

In the 1960's I spent several years working with and studying Civil Defense, etc. This product is an American Dream come true. It seems to me this is an answer to one's prayers as far as providing proper nutrition, with a minimum amount required and requiring very little storage space. If we ever get into a nuclear war, this could be the means of providing good nutrition to millions of people.

Rome, IL

Morning sickness leaves

I would like to join the large group of people singing the praises of Spirulina. I am in the 6th month of my third pregnancy and I have more energy than I did during my previous pregnancies. I also find that I require less sleep than I did before.

I have been taking Spirulina for a year and a half -- since the birth of my second child. When I became pregnant this time, I quit taking Spirulina because I didn't know if my doctor would approve of my taking it along with my prenatal vitamins. When I quit taking Spirulina I became very tired and began experiencing morning sickness. I decided to try taking just three tablets a day along with my prenatals and found that my energy level immediately increased, and my morning sickness ceased entirely.

Gresham, OR

I am writing this because I have heard that there are women who are concerned about the use of Spirulina during pregnancy. The only regret that I have concerning Spirulina use during the pregnancy of my second child was that I wish I had taken it from the very beginning of my pregnancy!

I started Spirulina when I was 5 months pregnant -- at the time I was slightly anemic and under considerable stress (single with another older child to care for, plus I was working full time on a swing shift schedule). Upon the addition of Spirulina to my diet, my energy increased and within 2½ to 3 months, my hematocrit went from 34.5 to 40.5 -- and this was done without iron supplements! I also used Spirulina and juice during the labor and continued using it while nursing my son.

I *highly* recommend its use to any women desiring a healthy, energetic pregnancy, as well as a healthy, strong child! My son was 9 lbs. at birth, crawled at 5 months, and continues to be exceptionally strong and well-developed for his age.

One recommendation I will make to pregnant/nursing women is that they drink lots of water in addition to the Spirulina, especially the first 3 months of pregnancy when constipation is more likely to occur.

I used 3 teaspoons daily with nothing but great results!!

Mt. View, CA

Chapter 2

WEIGHT LOSS

Thousands of people have lost weight, when all else has failed, after simply adding Spirulina to their diet. Why? One woman described her Spirulina diet experience like this: "I took 2 or 3 tablets of Spirulina 1/2 hour before each meal. I knew I was getting a complete supply of nutrients with the tablets, and it was as if my body recognized this right away, and sent a signal up to the brain to say, 'We're full.' I felt no need to eat and eat because my body was already satisfied."

However, despite the reports of thousands of consumers, the FDA prevents manufacturers from making weight loss claims for Spirulina.

Satisfied with about 1/2 the food . . .

For the past three weeks I have taken three [Spirulina] tablets before my noon meal daily and have found that my appetite is controlled so that I am satisfied with about 1/2 the food I would normally eat. In the three weeks I have gone from 180 lbs. to 167 lbs. To say the least, I am certainly satisfied with the results.

Santa Rosa, CA

I am thirty-four years old and am employed as a production control supervisor for a local foundry. During the past five or six years, a great many changes have taken place in my life, but only during the past several months have I come to realize that I needed more positive, self-controlled change. In seeking this change, I have encountered a group of people of like mind and spirit, one of whom, only ten days ago, introduced me to Spirulina. This woman, an instructor for a polarity balancing exercises workshop, suggested that I take six of the 500 mg. tablets 30 minutes prior to each meal as an appetite suppressor. I discovered that my consumption of food has been reduced by at least fifty percent. However, in addition to reducing my appetite, I have begun to notice an increase in my energy levels. I seem to have a feeling of increased well-being. I don't know if these changes are solely attributable to Spirulina or whether I can expect further changes, but I am sold.

Fort Worth, TX

I began taking Spirulina approximately 6 weeks ago. I took two tablets 20 minutes before each of my three meals and, believe me, it did definitely diminish my appetite — I lost 14 lbs. While I was losing this unwanted weight, I did not experience the usual weight losing symptoms, such as hunger, grouchiness, etc. Instead, while I was not feeling bad, I felt even better than before the Spirulina and the energy I now have seems to me at times to be almost unbelievable.

I would also like to add that, while my husband has no weight problem, he takes his Spirulina during or shortly after his meals and he also is experiencing the feeling of more energy and a greater degree of well-being.

St. Louis, MO

I have tried Spirulina plankton tablets and find them and [the Spirulina] book very exciting. I've been interested in health and foods for a number of years. This hit me as what I've been waiting for.

I lost 10 unwanted pounds within 2 weeks.

Cardiff, CA

"It costs me nothing to take Spirulina."

I am very happy with Spirulina.

I am taking 5 tablets before I break my fast and then I usually eat 1/2 of a grapefruit.

4 tablets in the middle of the morning and 4–6 at noon time. The ones at noon I sometimes take with some juice (apple or grape), 4–5 tablets in the middle of the afternoon, and 4 tablets before I eat my normal evening meal. The tablets that I take before my evening meal I take at least 45 min. prior.

I haven't felt as good as I feel now in years. I have lost 20 lbs. in less than 3 weeks. I have much more ambition and energy. I have had no problems at all with taking Spirulina. I also notice that I wake up in the mornings before the alarm goes off and am usually up an hour earlier than I was getting up before.

Several of my friends are taking Spirulina and all of them that are trying to lose weight have lost weight as long as they've remembered to take the Spirulina before they've eaten.

I have also come to the conclusion that IT COSTS ME NOTHING TO TAKE SPIRULINA. I am now taking Spirulina instead of the lunches that I was buying in the past. Lunch always cost me over $3.00, so I am actually saving several dollars per week. This is the same feeling that I get from my friends that take Spirulina—that it is free as you take it instead of junk food.

Niagara Falls, NY

I have taken 3 tablets [of Spirulina plankton] before each meal now for 2 months and feel more energy and my head feels clearer (easy to think). My appetite is not half as robust and as a result of this I've lost 10 lbs. and now have stabilized at 115 lbs. (which I haven't seen since I was 15!).

Coulterville, CA

"I was a skeptic. . . . I lost 31 pounds. . . ."

I was a skeptic, but no more. I used the plankton and protein foods (chicken, fish, eggs, cheese) when I needed to. I was not hungry— not a bit, and I lost 31 pounds in 5 weeks. I have 100 pounds more to lose, and I'm doing it using [Spirulina] plankton. I feel fantastic and am going to continue using the plankton after my weight goal is reached.

Florence, OR

My wife and I have been using the tablets and have lost approx. 25 lbs. and have gained a great deal of energy and stamina.

So. Gate, CA

I am presently on Spirulina tablets. I think they are great. I have been on the fast for a week and have lost numerous lbs., as well as having a feeling of well being. I have never had the empty or hungry feeling.

However, the first day was terrible. I had such a severe headache. I realize it was caffeine withdrawal and other toxins that were in my system. I have no intention of going back to coffee, sugar, "the nonsense foods." I am very happy with Spirulina and would like to sell it.

Mt. Vernon, OH

I have personally taken Spirulina, my wife has taken it and I have tested it alone, with food, with exercise and have stopped taking it for five days just to prove to myself that the Spirulina was causing what was going on within my body instead of some other outside influence which I was not aware of. I remarked to my wife and my cousin after the first week of Spirulina, "I don't know what is going on, but I don't want it to stop."

The reason I was so interested was that I have been grossly overweight all my life.

On August 17th, I started the Spirulina. The results were so amazing that I could not believe it myself. As of this morning, I weigh 189 lbs., about what I weighed when I was 10 years old.

Columbus, IN

On a day when I was fasting [with Spirulina plankton] I gave a pint of blood and felt no ill effects.

I had more energy when fasting. To give you an idea of how much: upon arising I jogged from 5 to 10 miles—then spent from 2½ to 3½ hrs. swimming from one end of a lake and back—tired, yes, but not exhausted—that's a lot of energy!

I have lost 22½ lbs. on Spirulina since I started 1 month ago and feel great.

Dallas, TX

I have been taking from 5–10 Spirulina tablets per day for almost 3 weeks. I feel great! I have much more energy and I've even noticed a mellowing of my energy level this past week. My appetite has been reduced to zilch! I used to eat from 7:30 AM to 11:00 PM. I've stopped eating breakfast and lunch. I only drink juice during the day, then I have dinner. I am going to start a protein sparing fast next week. I'm confident that I will begin to lose weight with Spirulina (I already lost 14 pounds!).

Detroit, MI

I've been taking Spirulina for seven weeks and have lost 45 lbs. I take six tablets ½ hour before each meal and if hungry I take another 2 or 3 between meals. I have more energy and I haven't had any bad effects. I've tried everything you can imagine before Spirulina and nothing worked.

Mill Valley, CA

Clear skin and sparkling eyes! . . .

I have successfully lost 37 pounds on this wonderful God-given nutrient [Spirulina]. I feel and look like a brand new person. My skin is clearer; my eyes sparkle in a beautiful clarity; and the step in my walk is strong, firm, and springy.

Seattle, WA

In 4 months I have lost 22 lbs. without being hungry or depriving myself. I now sleep an average of 2 hours less per night.

New York City, NY

I have lost 16 lbs. in the last month using Spirulina. People laughed at my "crazy diet" but now the Enquirer article is out everyone is asking me questions about Spirulina.

Captiva Island, FL

I have been using Spirulina for a week and I find it really good for me. I have lost a pound a day so far.

Los Gatos, CA

So many compliments!

I have been taking Spirulina for about 30 days.

I am quite pleased and have lost about 19 lbs. I was going to wait to write after I had lost 5 more pounds but changed my mind.

I am feeling so much better and had so many compliments. I decided to write now.

Inglewood, CA

[I] have been using the Spirulina on a diet to lose weight and have found it to be a life saver for me. I still tend to think it is too good to be true because I have had little success with dieting before, as everyone else does that has hypoglycemia. I lost 15 lbs. on it.

Midland, TX

On [X brand] Spirulina I've lost 6 pounds in one week, eating only a small amount of food—all without feeling fatigue or hunger. I love it and feel great.

Mill Valley, CA

The writer has been on Spirulina since January [1981] and am very pleased with the results. To date, I have lost approximately 20 lbs. and have great energy and feel twenty years younger. I have been constipated my entire life up until I started on Spirulina and now I am very regular and to boot I no longer have hemorrhoids, they have been completely gone for two months.

I recommend Spirulina to all my friends that want to feel better and have more energy. I am 58 years old and now weigh 133.5 pounds, thanks to [X brand] Spirulina.

Alamogordo, NM

Not tempted back to bad habits. . . .

I would like to express some of the wonderful changes that I have experienced since I have been using SPIRULINA. First, I have lost 30 lbs. that I have been trying to lose for about 10 years. With Spirulina the weight came off and I never once fought hunger pains or have been tempted to go back to my bad habits of eating anything in view. (THE WEIGHT STAYED OFF).

My allergies are alleviated through the use of [. . .]*, I have noticed my nose has stopped dripping and my eyes are open and no longer itch.

I have noticed the new hair coming back in the hairline at the temples is black and not grey. Forty-five days ago I began taking [. . .]*. I think this is the one that has credit for my hair growing back.

I had some age spots on the backs of my hands and arms that have now disappeared.

I have more energy and need less sleep than I ever have had in my entire life. Several of us have noticed an increase in our sex drive.

PRAISE THE LORD AND PASS THE SPIRULINA!!!

Fresno, CA

In July I had a heart attack followed by a stroke in November. Up to date I have lost 50 lbs. and I weighed 147 when I left the hospital.

I have a deep feeling that Spirulina will be the making of a new body for me. I take [Spirulina with bee pollen and ginseng] before meals.

Homeland, CA

It seems that everyone I know is either overweight, tired or a combination of both. I've had so many positive reactions and when time permits I'll write a list of testimonies.

I've lost 8 lbs. (need to lose about 15 more) and feel "fantastic." I take [Spirulina with comfrey, bee pollen, ginseng, and niacin.]

Houston, TX

I am interested in becoming a dealer for Spirulina.

I love [Spirulina] and I'm telling all my friends to get some. I think it is just the greatest thing for weight loss.

Necedah, WI

I am writing to let you know I am a new customer and I have been so excited over my results of Spirulina plankton that I just had to write. For years and years, I've had a weight problem with a very bad heart which meant the weight problem was a death toll around me; till one day I met a lady who told me about [Spirulina] and I know it was the answer I had been looking for. I had a stroke last November of '80 and a doctor said if I kept my weight down I would probably never have any more, so you can see why I am so excited. I've been on Spirulina now for a good [2] months and have lost 30 lbs. So I feel it was God leading me to [Spirulina] and will write again when I lose more. I started at 247 and am down to 217. I never feel hungry and want to thank you from the depth of my heart for [Spirulina].

P.S.   I have been making it a goal to help others to meet with Spirulina so they won't suffer as I have.

Homeland, CA

I've lost a total of 12 lbs. in 1 month on [Spirulina with trace minerals] also my complexion has cleared up (I have adult acne) and I have more energy than I've ever had. (I also work 3 jobs). So I do realize the advantages of being part of the Spirulina Family. I am going to be able to quit one of my jobs soon thanks to my Spirulina sales.

Diamond Springs, CA

From a husband and wife
delighted with weight and inches lost

My husband and I began taking Spirulina plankton, [with ginseng, bee pollen, and niacin], June 6, 1981. We were both 35 and 40 pounds overweight and had been unable to lose more than 4 or 5 pounds on any diet or program for quite a few years. We began by taking (1) [Spirulina with niacin tablet] daily, along with (2) [Spirulina with ginseng and bee pollen tablets] and (2) Spirulina Plankton tablets, three times daily about 40 to 60 minutes before each mealtime (whether we planned to eat or not). To our amazement we found (within about 36 hours) that our appetites had decreased and continued to decrease more each day, yet we had more energy and felt better and clearer headed each day. By June 13, 1981, I had lost 17 pounds, and my husband had lost about 20 pounds, (we both were also losing inches at the same time). At this time I realized that I had forgotten to take my hormone, allergy and high blood pressure pills for 4 or 5 days and my husband had forgotten his muscle spasm pills, high blood pressure and allergy pills also. We both started to take them, but it occurred to us that we felt better without them for that length of time so we did not begin taking them.

On July 5, 1981, I had lost 30 pounds and was wearing size 7–9 and I had to alter my husband's work and dress slacks from about a 39-inch waistband to a 37-inch one. By August 5th or so he came home from work to change into his dress slacks, took his belt off and his trousers almost fell to his knees. I had to purchase new slacks and work pants size 34–35 inches for him and size 5–6 clothes for myself. We were amazed that neither one of us were real wrinkled or had sagging skin anywhere since we had not had time to exercise.

Not wanting to lose or gain any more weight we both went on just a maintaining program of (1) plankton plus (2) [Spirulina with ginseng tablets] three times daily, about 45 minutes before each meal, along with (1) [Spirulina with niacin tablet] in the morning. This was fine for approximately 3 more weeks, then we both had to increase the number of tablets to (4) each of the plankton and (4) each of the [Spirulina with ginseng tablets] three times daily, about 45 minutes before each meal along with (1) [Spirulina with niacin tablet] in the A.M. and (1) around the noon hour. By September 15, I was taking (8) plankton and (6) [Spirulina with ginseng tablets] and (1) [Spirulina with niacin tablet] three times daily. This worked for three weeks and then I felt like I was slowly gaining weight. I decided to experiment with (2) plankton, (2) [Spirulina with ginseng tablets] (1) [Spirulina with niacin tablet] and (2) [Spirulina with trace minerals tablets], three times daily. I did this for 3 or 4 days then increased the plankton by two more, and the [Spirulina with ginseng tablets] by two more (3) times daily. It seems that my body would reach a plateau and I would either gain or just sit there for a day or so and the only way I could keep my weight where I wanted it was to just vary the number of plankton and [Spirulina with ginseng tablets] and take the same amount of any of the other tablets. I am still doing this, so is my husband, my distributors and many of my customers.

It appears to me and my distributors and customers and my husband that if you stay at any one level for any length of time the body becomes too accustomed to that and doesn't respond positively, until you change to another level — whether it's increasing or decreasing the amounts you are taking. This seemed to be true whether you became hungrier or not. It appears that everyone's metabolism is so different that you have to just experiment on yourself.

I would like to add that my husband and I and many of my distributors and customers did not change our diets drastically on our own. We did find that most of us could only eat between 3/4, 1/2 or 1/4 of what we had normally been eating. Our desire for sweets was drastically curbed and fruits seemed to taste better than candy, cake and cokes. Even when most of us went off the wagon, so to speak, we found that as a rule what we thought would really hit the spot didn't taste so good after all. We were all really amazed at that.

There are still some distributors and customers that did not lose but a few pounds and even a few gained a few pounds. As a rule though after casually questioning most of them, they would usually confess that they didn't take their tablets either at the right times or weren't taking the proper amounts so they could eat more if they went out to lunch, dinner, or to a party. Even a few would take them just whenever they remembered and many times it was a few minutes before or right after they had eaten. The ones who were made to realize that this was the program for skinny people to put weight on, and started taking the tablets in the correct amounts and at the right times, did realize some weight loss, some lost quite a number of pounds.

My experience has been so far that people who lost weight before going on the plankton program, especially if they had lost from 10 to 15, or even 20 pounds wanted to lose too fast whatever more they had decided they needed to lose and would not stay on the plankton long enough, or take the correct amounts. People who had one or more operations, especially women who had hysterectomies, and were on medications such as hormones, nerve pills, etc., had more trouble losing weight than most. The women that did stick with the right amounts of plankton, [Spirulina with ginseng] and [Spirulina with niacin] varying them up or down in amounts, for 10 weeks to 3 months or more did have pretty good results but they appeared to lose many more inches than actual pounds.

Most people including my husband and I were delighted with the way we felt as much as with the weight and inches we lost. We all enjoyed having twice as much energy as we had before taking the plankton, plus feeling great. It seemed to help me and my husband and many others think more clearly and we seemed to be able to handle irritating things more easily. We all loved the sense of well-being we attained, some after being on the plankton for a short time, others after a longer period of time. I also liked the fact that my husband's muscle "spasms" in his back and arms and legs have almost ceased entirely, plus my circulation has improved enough that my legs and arms don't feel numb and ache as before and my headaches are getting rarer, in fact I haven't had a migraine headache since the first month.

Ponca City, OK

She lost the craving for sweets

I started taking [Spirulina] plankton the 1st of July and it diminishes my appetite so that I eat a lot less, sometimes skipping two meals in a day and at the same time I feel better than I have in years. I seem to have more energy and do not tire even though I am doing more work. I also don't have the craving for sweets that I used to have, and it has regulated my elimination so that I no longer have to take anything to add bulk to my diet as I did in the past. I have lost 14 lbs. since I started taking it and feel so good about myself.

Murphy, ID

Spirulina is fabulous. I have 5 different colored tee-shirts to wear with **SPIRULINA MAMA** on the front. I get lots of comments on them. I also made the **WALL OF FAME** at the gym. Lost over 15 lbs. on a 23 day fast, 9¼". Never felt so good - thanks to Spirulina.

Norwalk, CT

I have just completed taking my first bottle of [Spirulina] and feel fantastic. I have lost ten pounds, have increased energy and best of all have a suppressed appetite without hunger pangs for the first time in my life.

Lake Oswego, OR

I have been on Spirulina plankton for one week now and I have lost 10 pounds. I feel terrific and have noticed an increase in energy. I am very much overweight and have noticed since being on [Spirulina] that I am eating much less and do not have the desire for junk foods or anything else that isn't good for the body, such as diet soft drinks.

Salt Lake City, UT

I am so thankful [for] Spirulina. I cannot express my joy enough. I have lost 21 lbs. in 5 weeks. I have tried to lose weight all my life and I get very sick with headaches and sick at my stomach when I don't eat. But most of all I get so cranky, you just can't stand to be around me. But not with Spirulina! I have no hunger at all. People always say, "You have such a pretty face but can't you do something about your weight?"

Spirulina is my answer; my way of eating is changing. I never cared for apples but sure loved candy bars. Now I crave apples and fruit and can't eat candy at all.

More than just the weight is gone: I've lost many inches, two dress sizes, and that's a fact.

Fresno, CA

From a "former fatso" with high blood pressure

My wife and I have been using Spirulina now for over a year and I must say the benefits derived from a regular use of this wonderful food surpassed our greatest expectations.

When I began using Spirulina I was weighing 215 lbs. and jogging a slow but regular 10 minute mile. My wife could not even do this without experiencing angina chest pains. In fact, our family doctor was insisting on sending her to a specialist.

After taking the [Spirulina with niacin tablets] and 100% Plankton tablets for approx. six months, I noticed a new surge of natural energy taking hold of my entire body. [My wife] began jogging and much to our joy, she runs regularly without experiencing chest pains at all. My weight has come down to 180 lbs and my blood pressure is normal and we both participate in races. [My wife] ran her first race last October and won first place in her age bracket (over fifty). This was a three mile race. I have been running regularly this year and have participated in fourteen races ranging from three to ten miles. My time ranges from an eight min. mile to seven and a half. I know this isn't setting the woods on fire but when you consider a former fatso with high blood pressure who is fifty six years age and who had never run a race in his life; I think it is pretty good!

Rome, IL

"I really do feel like a new person because I AM."

April 26th, 1981, I weighed 280 pounds, being only 5'8"; obviously I was overweight. I was tired, had high blood pressure and was extremely irritable at times. I'm owner-operator of two bakeries and coach at the varsity level at our local high school. I'm married and have five children and in the lay ministry of The Church of Jesus Christ of Latter Day Saints.

April 27, I started taking the Spirulina tablets. I took two to three tablets three times a day for the first week, then four tablets per meal for the duration. I existed on Spirulina for a total period of fifty-six days, taking only natural veg/fruit juices and of course water.

The second day I experienced some severe headaches and stomach cramps from, more than likely, withdrawing from normal food, but from that point on I could literally feel no hunger and actually no desire for food. All headaches went away, not even the slightest feeling of one coming on. Previously it was two per day! The tired feeling was leaving rapidly, as well as the pounds. I could write a book and lecture throughout America on what Spirulina did for my health. I lost *eighty pounds* in fifty-six days, blood pressure dropped from over 200/100 to 122/78. Every test blood, heart and urine proved excellent, actually superb, and completely amazed my doctor.

At no time after the second day did I feel weak, hungry or irritable. The only experience I felt was a desire to chew on something, which I didn't. I gained unbelievable vitality from the second day on, but more important is that it changed my life mentally, physically and spiritually. I really do feel like a new person because I AM.

Hot Springs, SD

I took Spirulina tablets and was very happy with the results. I lost 13 lbs. in 6 days by fasting and only taking your tablets and fruit juice. I felt good and worked hard every day. I could think more clearly and after the first day, wasn't hungry.

College Grove, TN

I am writing you this letter to tell you of my wonderful 28 day juice fast with Spirulina. I first tried [Spirulina] at a health convention in March of last year. But the friend of mine who turned me on to [it] moved to Phoenix and has worked and lived with [a renowned wholistic health practitioner]. Well, after Christmas after destroying my colon health through abusive eating and drinking, my weight shot up to 201 lbs. of fat and poison. I had to do an enema every 3 days—this consisted of tea made with Red Raspberry leaves and Spirulina.

So after 28 days I lost 20 lbs. of fat—I work out at a Nautilus Fitness Center and the results I have had in the last 6 weeks are phenomenal. I have gained about 3 lbs. of muscle in my upper back and shoulders. The workouts I do are brief but are in true Nautilus principles. Some machines, I went up 3 plates in a month. I attribute this to Spirulina due to the fact I've worked out there 3 years and thought I'd reached my peak.

Lowell, IN

On taking Spirulina for three weeks I lost 20 pounds of ugly fat. I felt great, slept well and have a greatly improved disposition.

Mill Valley, CA

"God answered my prayers"

I have been fat for 40 of my 53 years and know the heartbreak that goes with it. I have lost and gained over and over. I've tried everything even when it was dangerous. I'm not alone. Most of the women in my TOPS club are the same as me.

3 or 4 years ago I was tested for hypoglycemia and put on a diet for it. I still shook inside, was always hungry, even after a large meal, and still went on sugar binges that would nearly kill me. My blood pressure had been low for years and now it went high, so I was really scared and desperate for help.

I went to an endocrinologist. He told me the reason I shook inside and was hungry all the time was that the hypoglycemia caused my stomach to empty too fast. He put me on a diet with pills to slow the stomach down. I still shook inside, I still had sugar binges but now had a new problem, I was deathly ill. I called the doctor and told him. He said the pills could not make me ill and I had to be on them, so I started taking them again. I stopped and started several times and it was always the same, so I finally decided the cure was worse than the disease, and stopped taking the pills.

I kept trying diets but the inner shaking and binges were in control and by January '81, I was heavier than I had ever been. For the first time in my life I really looked old. Fat and 50 was really hard to take.

From January to April '81, I lost 20 pounds and spent the summer trying to keep it off. By September I was losing the battle and had gained six pounds back. I was thinking suicide all the time and was so tired that moving around would exhaust me. I didn't know what I was apt to do and was afraid of my depression, so for the first time in my life prayed to God for help with my weight. I had always felt my weight was disgusting and not worthy of God's attention, but there was nowhere else to go.

A few days after praying for help, I decided to read a book, and a book that had been lying around for years seemed to leap at me, so I read it. As I read, my self-esteem grew and all the questions I had been asking doctors for years were being answered. The book is Dr. Atkins Diet Revolution Book. PLEASE DON'T QUIT READING -- THE BEST IS YET TO COME!

Two days after reading the Atkins book I heard about Spirulina but was too involved with the Atkins diet to pay any attention. From the beginning I felt good on the Atkins diet. I have taken vitamins for years so was not concerned about any lack of nutrients from not eating fruit and carbohydrates. I couldn't believe it when the shaking in my stomach stopped and then the binges. The only problem was I didn't lose any weight. Three weeks after being on the diet I started taking Spirulina I bought at the health food store. Six weeks later, feeling better but still no weight loss, I followed my sister's advice and started taking [X brand] Spirulina. I started taking it Sept. 14/81 and as of today, Nov. 23/81 have lost 23 lbs! More important than the weight loss is how good I feel and look. I have 70 lbs. to lose but I know it is going. Most of my family and friends are now on it and having the same good results.

My husband started on the Spirulina supplements too as he has a poor tolerance of sugar also. He wasn't trying to lose weight but has lost from 182 to 170. He is 59 and for years has always had to eat on time or he got all nervous and jittery. He now spends hours hunting and tracking without getting the shakes. Being on vitamins for years, we are both impressed with the energy boost we have since starting Dr. Hills' program.

I know God answered my prayers by showing me why I'm fat through Dr. Atkins and how to lose it through Dr. Hills. I follow Dr. Atkins type diet, only eat less of it and supplement with Spirulina products. For any bowel problems I take soy bran tablets (6 per meal).

When I started this program I was taking diet pills, diuretics, proloid, and hormones. I no longer take any of them. I don't know why I no longer need them and wish you could explain it to me.

Three weeks after starting the Spirulina I went on a fast. I followed directions and had no problems. I bowled, worked, drove the car, had no weak spells or hypoglycemia attacks. IT WAS FANTASTIC! I have never been able to skip a meal without eating it along with my next meal. The only problem I had was well-meaning friends that thought I would get sick.

Mt. Vernon, OH

She maintains a lower weight while eating what she wants

I have been using Spirulina since March 23, 1981, and am extremely satisfied with the results of increased energy, physical well-being and maintaining a 20 pound weight loss.

In the beginning I fasted on Spirulina for eight days and lost 10 pounds with no feeling of hunger or weakness. I was able to continue my normal busy schedule with plenty of energy and mental clarity - really feeling good, better than usual.

During the next three weeks I was able to lose another 10 lbs. by eating either Spirulina tablets or powder regularly and skipping one meal a day. Again, I felt no hunger and had plenty of energy. I also found I did not want as much to eat at meals and did not crave sweets and between meal snacks as I had previously.

Since March I have maintained a weight of 130 pounds compared to 150 pounds before that, while eating what I want. I am 51 years old and 5 feet 6 inches tall.

Another interesting and wonderful observation is that I have had no diverticulitis attacks since I began eating [. . .]* and the arthritis in my shoulder and hand has disappeared. I spent 1/3 to 1/2 my time on antibiotics for diverticulitis before March 23. You may confirm this with internist Dr. . . . in Atlanta, if you wish.

Woodstock, GA

Better weight distribution

I have been taking vitamins and other health products for many years. I thought that they were fine but they didn't seem to do anything for me, although I felt better (just thinking that I was taking vitamin supplements). I have always been an active person. I have been involved in a lot of athletic activities, mainly weight lifting which takes a lot of protein to help build the muscles (firm and tone) and a lot of other nutrients to purify and detoxify the blood while building new blood cells. I have found that I didn't always have the energy I needed to complete my workout. Now, I can take my [. . .]*, and get my energy and protein (all at once) while getting all the nutrients I need. I also don't eat regularly, or the right things, so this really is needed to be healthy and happy. I've felt so much better and healthier since I've been using Spirulina. I'm very happy selling Spirulina and I would recommend it to everyone.

We both are enjoying selling and using Spirulina. Everyone that has bought Spirulina is feeling better and are so glad that we had made them aware of the wonderful Spirulina.

I have lost 1–2 inches around the waist and my weight has been distributed correctly, such as my arms, chest, etc. My weight has only decreased 5 lbs.

Roseville, MN

Spirulina is fantastic! We tried the powder in juice. I felt an immediate burst of energy! I have never felt that before. My mind felt so clear. [A friend] also felt the energy and noticed the difference right away. We both have always taken vitamins every day for years. We both have also been *very* concerned about our health. I have also been concerned about my weight.

None of the vitamins seemed to do anything for us, like Spirulina has! We originally purchased 100 tabs Spirulina plankton on April 24th. Went back on May 8th and purchased 200 tabs Spirulina, 4 oz. powder, [and the Spirulina with bee pollen and ginseng combination.] We have been making large purchases on a regular basis ever since.

Before I was concerned about my health and nutrients, it was only how heavy I was. I went on a 3-month fast, hardly eating anything. I went from 118 lbs. to 89 lbs. I was always tired and run down. I gained it all back in 5 months.

I have been in many physical activities such as figure skating, Karate, jogging. I have a lifetime membership at the Health Spa since 1978. I'm involved in a 6-day workout which includes yoga, weight lifting, jogging, swimming, floor exercises, aerobics, dance classes. I have used cellulite machines, cellulite creams, diet pills, plastic sweat suits and anything I heard of to lose pounds. Nothing worked at all, except I lose weight by not eating.

April 1981, I started using Spirulina. I felt the energy within 5–10 minutes after I drank the powder and juice. I have experienced not being tired, having a lot of energy. I don't have hunger pains all the time and the want for sugar. My thoughts are a lot more clean and my attitude towards life is all changed. My world is a wonderful world because I feel better about myself and people in my life. Spirulina has helped my physical and mental being. I now have the energy to last through a long 6 hours workout daily, without having to have instant energy (sugar) afterwards.

I started using Spirulina in April. I had not metabolized correctly since my weight loss 1978. [Now] I have the natural menstruation period flow correctly May, June, July, August and September. I have lost 15 lbs. in the first 3 months (eating 1500 calories). I have tried fasting 5 days, 2 days and 2 days, total of 9 days. I loved the energy.

I feel great! Thanks to Spirulina, I feel young and renewed, a new person.

Roseville, MN

Please allow me the opportunity to thank you for introducing me to [X brand] Spirulina. I honestly believe it is the best supplement I have ever taken. Let me tell you why.

Having always had a weight problem, I have tried many diets. Some were successful, some were not. This always resulted in the yo-yo syndrome. I would lose 20 pounds only to gain back 15. Then lose 5 pounds and gain back 20.

When I began taking Spirulina, I found that controlling calorie intake was much easier. Not only that, but I never feel tired or all dragged out. Neither do I ever experience that jittery, jumpy high that comes from diet pills.

Philadelphia, PA

Overwhelmed

I want to thank you for introducing me to [X brand]. Having tried and failed at numerous other weight loss programs, I am now a successful dieter. Not only have I lost 29 lbs. of unwanted body weight, I have lost inches off my waist and thighs. All of this in only six weeks and without starving or hunger pangs! As an extra bonus I am looking and feeling better than I have in years. The tablets work for me as an appetite suppressant but without any ill effects. The overall effect has been overwhelming.

There is no secret to my success these last weeks. I haven't set out to crash diet, I have simply cut out eating the obviously fattening and non-nutritious foods, I exercise 15 minutes daily and I take 3–4 tablets 4 times a day. The amazing aspect of my current diet is that I have never been able to do this and stick with it, because I have always become discouraged by the side-effects of pills or constant hunger! (It) gives me a "full feeling", even on the days I eat poorly, and I continue to lose - without those horrid hunger pangs.

I am a person who needed help to diet, I found that in [X brand]; I will continue to use it even after I reach my weight goal because the high energy level I have now is one I will always want.

Philadelphia, PA

Chapter 3

HYPOGLYCEMIA AND OTHER SPECIAL DISEASES

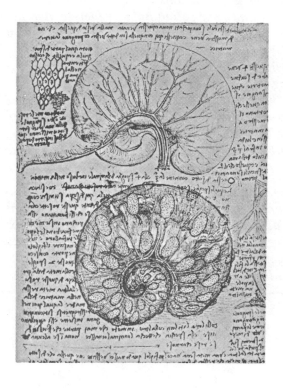

In these times when the person of average income has a better standard of living than the king or queen of 500 years ago, it comes as a surprise to us that many of the diseases prevalent in today's society are nutritionally based. Yet more and more, research reveals that this is so. The depleted soils in which our food is grown, and the ravages of stress and poor eating habits which render our internal organs incapable of proper digestion and absorption, contribute to a deficiency of the nutrients our bodies depend on. Users of Spirulina, who are benefiting from its nutritional power, report the alleviation of an amazing variety of disease symptoms, common and *uncommon in our society today. Gathered here you will find letters regarding hypoglycemia, hepatitis, arthritis, multiple sclerosis, asthma, allergies, diabetes, bursitis, cystic fibrosis, agent orange, high blood pressure, and others, all written by users of Spirulina. They have a story to tell.*

*(*Editor's Note: *These letters represent the opinions of the users themselves. FDA regulations prevent manufacturers or distributors of Spirulina products from making medical claims for this food. Distributors are allowed, however, to relate their personal experience with the products. Spirulina is not a drug or a medicine but a nutritious food. It is a supplement and people should not stop using their prescribed medications without their doctor's advice.)*

From a hypoglycemic

After taking Spirulina Plankton for two weeks, while continuing my normal diet, I noticed that my cravings for sweets and carbohydrates diminished radically. As a diagnosed functional hypoglycemic, sugar has been the biggest deterrent to maintenance of my ideal weight and energy levels. A major symptom created by this condition was afternoon tiredness, which had become more the norm than the exception for me. During the first three days on Spirulina, the tiredness seemed to increase. But I persisted—knowing that natural (homeopathic) remedies often seem to intensify symptoms temporarily—and from the fifth day until the present (2 months later), my energy level has been high and stable.

These effects so excited me that I went on a cleansing fast, which involved 1 teaspoon of Spirulina in 8–10 ounces of vegetable or fruit juice three times a day and in between "meals" a mixture of 1 tablespoon of fresh lemon juice, 1 tablespoon of pure maple syrup and 10 ounces of water. After four days, I eliminated the lemonade mixture. I stayed on the Spirulina/juice fast for 20 days. During that time, I experienced:
—eradication of hay fever symptom
—no hypoglycemic symptoms
—no hunger
—increased energy
—the ability to carry on my normal work with greater efficiency
—greater ability to concentrate -- with increased clarity of mind
—natural elimination ([. . .]* is a natural detoxifier)
—deeper meditations
—shiny hair
—stronger, more supple fingernails
—less need for sleep
—a sense and aura of well-being
AND loss of 19½ pounds.

I've continued taking Spirulina after ending the fast and have been able to sustain the weight loss and the other effects, too.

Mill Valley, CA

After suffering from hypoglycemia for nearly fifteen years, during which doctors said "there was nothing wrong" with me, I stumbled upon an ad for Spirulina in a local newspaper. What a discovery! I've been taking it for three months and feel better than ever before! Keeping up with two preschool boys really puts [. . .]* to the test, but it never fails to supply me with enough energy to outlast my boys, and still have enough left for my husband and myself! I teach a women's fitness and aerobic dance class at the local YMCA, and I would be delighted to introduce some of the women to [this] amazing product.

Ottawa, IL

Constant tiredness has disappeared

During the last four months of use [of Spirulina], I have experienced my health greatly improve. Most significantly, my energy level has been sustaining a constancy that I have longed for. For nine years I have had many symptoms and problems due to hypoglycemia. I have felt tired much of the time and have had many headaches. Since using 3 tsp. of Spirulina powder daily, my headaches are gone and my constant tiredness has disappeared! I am *very* grateful for this nutritional product.

In addition, my appetite has decreased and I have been able to lose weight as well as fast on juice and Spirulina for up to 11 days, while still feeling terrific.

I also have many friends and am not at all shy - especially when I am sold on something: I'll be telling many more about Spirulina, you can be sure - (I love to convert sheep to shepherds!)

Ft. Lauderdale, FL

I am so thrilled with Spirulina plankton. I have hypoglycemia and have never fasted more than *6 hours* -- due to fainting spells from lack of protein. I fasted for 8 days and "forced" myself to eat fruit on day 9. My appetite is gradually returning – but only for natural foods -- no junk. I am happier and 7 lbs. lighter. I am taking it day by day.

All of my friends are excited and I want everyone to experience this.

Escondido, CA

Her doctor recommended Spirulina

I have been a Spirulina distributor now for a little over three months and am very proud to be one. I have suffered for quite a long time with no energy, severe headaches and I would have terrible weak spells.

The symptoms sounded like hypoglycemia. So, he [the doctor] ran the tests and sure enough I was suffering from a pretty severe case of hypoglycemia. He put me on a high protein diet and asked if I'd like to try Spirulina. That was the first I had ever heard of it.

I was pretty skeptical, as I have tried vitamins and didn't get any results, but I have faith in our doctor and he thought they would help, so I decided to give them a try. I started taking [Spirulina with ginseng, bee pollen, and niacin] on a Friday. We had guests come in from California to spend a week with us. By the following Monday morning I was feeling fantastic. I took our guests sight-seeing the whole week they were here and really felt like I was on top of the world. I still feel great, better than I have in twelve years or so. Even when I have a cold virus I don't lose my energy. It's absolutely marvelous. And no false high or dopey feelings from drugs. It's great.

My husband wanted to lose weight, but always got real tired out when he would try to diet. He's a pipefitter and does a lot of walking, etc. He's been finding it hard to get through the day. Was just worn out all the time and had terrible leg cramps at the end of the day. They would ache so bad a lot of nights that he wouldn't be able to sleep. After he saw what Spirulina did for me, he started taking them. In less than three weeks he had lost from a 36" waistline down to a 33" and is still losing and feeling great. He has all the energy he needs and absolutely no leg cramps any more.

We have our five year old son on 100% plankton. It has helped his appetite and I know it helps him have a balanced diet.

Last month, my mother-in-law came out and spent a couple of weeks with us. My mother-in-law is very overweight and has had four or five surgeries in the past few years. Because of the surgeries on her stomach she hasn't been able to have a normal bowel movement. She's had to force every b.m. she's had for over a year. The doctors haven't given her any hope of it ever being any different. Also, she has a bleeding ulcer on the outside of her body, has had it for nearly a year and when she got here it was bleeding quite badly.

We started her taking Spirulina the day she arrived. She had a regular and normal b.m. every day and the ulcer has stopped bleeding. The doctors had said, surgery was all that would help the ulcer, but it had stopped bleeding and wasn't hurting her. And she hadn't had a regular, normal b.m. in over a year. Needless to say, Spirulina went back home with them.

Surely no one would have to wonder why I'm a Spirulina distributor. My husband and I are completely sold on it and are doing all we can to tell others about it.

Oracle, AZ

"I feel better on the stuff."

Personally using [X brand]* - from the very first portion - I experienced results and continue to reap results. I cannot function normally without my daily supply. Having hypoglycemia, I have never known a pleasant and complete way of controlling it. For me, [X brand]* works!

The following is a testimonial from my daughter — which came to me as a complete surprise. "I have found by taking Spirulina that it is all true and I stand behind it 100%. [My husband] is telling all his friends about it and already two of them bought some. [His] boss is even asking about them! [He] went through the toxic backflush scene really heavily. Chills, tired, nervously anxious, jittery and aching bones — but with lots of energy. He swore he'd never take them again. So I read up really well on the "cleansing" phase and explained it to him. He said that was garbage and didn't take them that whole day. By the following morning I saw him quietly take his usual dosage and he meekly said, 'I feel better on the stuff.' So now you have it."

[My son] even noticed a noticeable mood change for the better, in his dad and so did I and so did [he] himself. He said he feels calmer. I am wondering about children's dosages.

Englewood, FL

Spirulina has truly changed my life! I have always been a very active person but at the same time have continually felt great fatigue. A few years ago I was diagnosed hypoglycemic, and that being a start, I think I have tried just about every kind of diet there is! Fasting was out of the question until now -- with the help of Spirulina. I am feeling much better -- less tired, less depressed, and much lighter. I have been telling everyone about it, even strangers in stores, and they all express a great interest. People at the Co-op, at my dance classes, at my health spa, art classes — it is amazing.

Indialantic, FL

In 1958 I developed a sugar problem. Through various tests (6 hour glucose tolerance, etc.) a treatment and diets were prescribed. This year my problem has become very acute. In searching for help, I came across Dr. Christopher Hills' book *Rejuvenating the Body through Fasting with Spirulina Plankton*.

I followed the instructions on the fast. I used only tomato and carrot juice in conjunction with Spirulina plankton for the first 14 days and lost 13 pounds. I then started eating salads and drinking carrot juice. On rising, I take the juice of a lemon in warm water. It is now 30 days since I began this program and I have lost 20 pounds.

I am now taking 3 teaspoons of [Spirulina] powder, 6 tablets of [Spirulina with comfrey and pepsin] and 6 tablets of [Spirulina with powdered marine shells]. I was never hungry, did not lose my energy, and have kept my muscle tone.

Albuquerque, NM

"This stuff really works!!"

One [friend] was kind enough to give me a sample and it has been the only effective food supplement in a treatment of chronic hepatitis that I have yet encountered. (I have had this condition for ten years). Praise God!! This stuff really works!!

Big Sur, CA

This friend is really being helped by the [. . .]* and it is because of him we have become involved. He was given a blood transfusion when having a kidney stone removed two years ago and the blood gave him the very worst type of *hepatitis* for which there is no known medical cure, chronic non-A, non-B type. Last year the doctors prescribed heavy doses of cortisone which he refused to take and went instead to a health clinic and is on a very strict diet. The medical profession told his wife he would be alive for only a short time. However, with the help of the Lord and good nutrition he is holding his own, his blood count has improved slightly. When I read how [. . .]* helped people with hepatitis, I went immediately to visit him and gave him some to take. Five days after taking it, he went for some tests and there was already some improvement as the [. . .]* had speeded up the toxin removal. He still has pains in his joints, etc. (which the doctors say are terminal signs - but they have been saying this for months). THE HEPATITIS HAS NOT YET BECOME CIRRHOSIS, so I really think [. . .]* will help.

Stuart, FL

I have been using the Spirulina tablets for a while now and have found that in general, my system has been working better than ever before. I started taking them due to a hepatitis condition I developed last year.

Westbury, NY

I have found that the ggx* tablets are good for arthritis. When I take the tablet I have very little trouble with arthritis. When I don't take the tablet for a while I have a lot of trouble with arthritis.

Has anyone else found this to be true?

Hopeville, GA

Arthritis is 75% gone . . .

I think [Spirulina] is wonderful. Have had painful arthritis for 45 years. Am thankful to say, 75% of it is gone. I've fasted for 35 days and feel great. We have a lot to thank Jehovah God for.

Phoenix, AZ

I discovered [. . .]* nearly a year ago through [the] wonderful book *Rejuvenating the Body through Fasting with Spirulina Plankton*. . . . Since then, I have derived great benefit from [the] suggestions and have alleviated allergy symptoms and pains from rheumatism and arthritis.

I consider [. . .]* to be essential, not only for these therapeutic purposes, but also as a daily nutritional supplement.

New York, NY

"My arthritis was so much better."

I have had stomach problems with digestion all my life of 62 years. Since taking [X brand] Spirulina my stomach has been so much better and I even lost 17 lbs. in weight. I have had thyroid problems with a heart valve problem too. Now I feel so much better, and of course, I am overweight, so [X brand] algae is just what I need.

I also have had arthritis very bad the last five years. It is in all my joints, so the doctor says, but mostly hip, hands, ankles, and back. I have days that I'm unable to get up and down and am unable to write. For the seven weeks I was taking [X brand] Spirulina, my arthritis was so much better and I had some days of happy enjoyment.

I bought [the] book *Rejuvenating the Body*. I think it's very very informative and truthful, as I can tell by my own experience.

Altus, OK

As a vegetarian, Spirulina is a Godsend, being my prime source of protein. I'm sure this is true of others as well.

As for what [. . .]* has done for me, aside from feeling better, I've become a walking advertisement in that I've lost about 12–15 lbs. and co-workers have commented on my more youthful appearance. One friend repeatedly tells me that he thinks if it hadn't been for [. . .]* he'd be dead. That's an exaggeration of course. But he's lost about 20 lbs. and claims that his hemorrhoids have disappeared and that his wrist and fingers are not as painful. Another friend troubled with arthritis and who was taking up to 20 aspirins a day said, but not to me, that he was delighted to awake one morning free from pain. One woman about 64 said after taking a bottle of [Spirulina with niacin] that she no longer gets tired at work after 10 hours a day. She's been eating it now about 3 months and although she won't say how much she has lost, it appears to me to be around 30 lbs. A neighbor, 84, likes it because her bowel movements are easy and regular.

St. Paul, MN

Gout symptoms gone

I am enclosing two of the latest articles about Spirulina. The one from November/December [1981] issue of The Health Quarterly is the finest article I have yet seen on the subject. But the other one, a one-page article, is also illuminating, especially because it reports what many doctors have now begun to say about Spirulina.

Just about everything said by them, I have either experienced or seen happen myself. Plus more! I was originally cautious (but not really skeptical) about accepting [. . .]* but I am 1,000% convinced through direct experience and observation about its value and efficacy as super nutrition that not only guards health but corrects bodily conditions and problems which stem from nutritional deficiency or abuse.

The best proof is myself. I suffered all last year from a painful left foot that was diagnosed as being due to "peripheral neuralgia." This began in February and continued until January this year. In the fall I found out, finally, that it was arthritic gout. A pain-killing anti-inflammatory drug, Indocin, was prescribed for me.

This helped to control the symptoms (pain and swelling) but, on the other hand, it kicked up an ulcer (in the pyloric channel between stomach and duodenum) which I had previously brought under control — typical Catch-22 situation caused by medication which attacks a certain problem but also produces a bad side effect. In December I started to take allopurinol (brand name Zyloprim) which reduces the uric acid level in the blood that brings on gout. But this, in turn, could cause kidney stones to form. At the same time I had to contend with the ulcer. Frankly, in December–January, I was in a real fix physically.

[A friend] introduced me to Spirulina on Xmas Eve. It wasn't until the last week in January that I began using Spirulina. I felt I had nothing to lose, and the literature I read made perfect sense to me.

. . . The gout is GONE!!! No more pain in the left foot, and I can jump and hop around on it! And I quit taking allopurinol in early February. My stomach is still sensitive, and I have to watch it, but I am not taking ulcer medicine. I can now work on the ulcer problem without having to contend with gout at the same time.

Gout is a nutritional and circulatory disease. The key organ in this is the liver, which controls the absorption of toxins as well as nutrients. My liver had not been in good shape, due to heavy drinking in the past and improper eating habits. True confession. [. . .]* has restored its functions, and this in turn has made the gout disappear. THERE IS ABSOLUTELY NO OTHER POSSIBLE EXPLANATION FOR THIS DRAMATIC IMPROVEMENT. My food has been lean (since the bypass operation in 1976), and it hasn't changed. The only thing that has changed is the Spirulina that I now take — 9–12 tablets a day. Yes, I am *not* today what I was 2 months ago. I am far more energetic, also, and my vision has improved. I could not, for example, read the newspaper without reading glasses. Today I can, if I have to. The vision without glasses is not perfect, but the words are visible. Often in the past, when driving on the freeway, the landscape would shimmer. Now it doesn't! And my thinking is much clearer and better. My appetite is good, but I don't eat as much and if I get hungry I don't feel weakened by it. My weight has gone down to 148–149 from 152–154 lbs.

San Francisco, CA

More energy for multiple sclerosis victim

I have multiple sclerosis, "M.S.". I started taking [. . .]* in June and it has sure helped me. . . .

I can't really afford it but it makes me feel so much better. I have been in a wheelchair for ten years and this [. . .]* gives me energy to get through the day and keep my house clean and livable.

Coalinga, CA

I am a 46–year old woman and weigh 82 lbs.

I have had lateral sclerosis for the past four years. I have reached the stage where I can only walk a few steps if someone holds me, and I do not have the use of my hands or arms.

I have a green vegetable drink every day as well as 1 TAB. of Spirulina every day. I have used the [. . .]* for three months and it gives me much more energy. If I took it after 4 p.m. I was awake most of the night. I have been out of it for about three weeks and I noticed the difference in my energy.

Phoenix, AZ

"I am slowly putting my long lost golf and tennis games together . . ."

As of September I began taking [X brand] Spirulina.

Three months later I am unbelievably experiencing the following:
1) After 18 years of only dreaming I would be able to walk distances again, I am walking 1 mile a day in 25 brief minutes;
2) Riding my indoor bicycle 3 miles - 10 minutes;
3) I am out slowly putting my long lost golf and tennis games together - which is tough - but I am so grateful to have the newly found energy, returning coordination, slowly returning strength of legs, arms, etc.;
4) No more overwhelming fatigue which required naps twice a day.

Why is [. . .]* working? Dr. . . . feels it is the pure 71% protein that's available, added to my usual good non-toxic diet -- a shot of health all systems are able to accept and to which there is response.

Of course, you can understand why I am so excited about it. To me, it's a miraculously perfect food - not a supplement. It is loaded with all the nutrients a body needs - can be used as basic diet food when one needs to lose weight. I could go on - but - with 100% protein available and nutrients enough to control my hypoglycemia symptoms as well as my MS picture, I am a new person!

Yoga classes are thriving too as they combine Yoga, good nutrition and Spirulina!

Totally, . . . [. . .]* has powerful healing and preventive medicine energies.

The doctor with whom I am associated, ... , M.D., is considering incorporating it in MS and all therapeutic programs.

Leucadia, CA

"Within 4 weeks I bought myself a mini-trampoline"

Since childhood I've been terribly bothered with *hay fever*, you know, the sneezing runny nose, burning eyes, and along with the hay fever I have a disease (I don't know the medical name) of the eyes. The doctor told me it was granulated eyelids. My eyelids always were red and itchy, like I had been crying, and also had dry white flakes on them which would make my eyelids itch badly and along with this, as an adult, I've had trouble with a continual dripping nose. Think that's bad? Not really, read on.

Twelve years ago I was diagnosed as having Multiple Sclerosis.

A year ago this February I became acquainted with Spirulina and after having heard how it had helped other people, thought I would give it a try and even signed up as a distributor, because if it was as good as I was told I would like to let people know. With M.S. I can't work but I can talk.

Like I said, a year ago this February I started taking Spirulina and was I ever surprised! Within 4 weeks I bought myself a mini-trampoline to exercise on; I was feeling so good. No, Spirulina has not cured me of M.S. but sure helps me feel better.

I have since made a move back to Arkansas to live with my parents, a move I would have never thought about before because of the hay fever, but I have not had *any* problems with hay fever since taking Spirulina, and no more red itching or flaking eyes. It's like a miracle.

I thank God for Spirulina. Oh yes, no more runny nose either.

I am not through yet. My 19 year old son has had trouble with pimples; even medication didn't help but [. . .]* has cleaned up his face of the pimples. Also he had a sinus problem and that has been cleared up.

Grape Vine, AR

Since I began taking [X brand] Spirulina I have noticed an overall increase in energy and endurance. I now average 5 to 6 hours of sleep, a night, getting up between quarter of 5 and 5 a.m. and working a very active and intense schedule until late at night, 6 days a week. My appetite for other food has decreased so I usually eat less than before -- I have been more fulfilled with Spirulina.

As a result of regular usage of [. . .]* I have enjoyed diminishing symptoms of asthma and related allergies which I have had since childhood. I am confident that this healing process will soon result in a complete cure.

I cannot conceive of ever wanting to stop using Spirulina and related products. My life has changed for the better in a deep and dramatic way. I feel compelled to share my enthusiasm with others so that they might be similarly benefitted.

Tucson, AZ

Help in fighting a 29 year old battle of hayfever

It wasn't long until I realized that for the first time in fighting a twenty-nine year old battle with hayfever that [. . .]* carried the promise of clearing it up for good. I had spent hundreds of dollars and tried every healing modality known to man, MDs, osteopaths, chiropractors, herbs, vitamins, diets, fasts (even wrote and published our book on the subject . . .) – but whatever I did had only temporary results.

Now, after four months, the longest period I ever went without the nauseating symptoms (that nearly cost me my job of court reporter on two occasions), I know that it is finally licked, thanks to [. . .]*. My guess is that it is because of the high protein content of the [. . .]*. We believe that because of our eleven years on a 100% raw food diet we were protein starved. My wife has had a remarkable improvement in her health as well.

My hayfever, incidentally, was not a sporadic springtime phenomenon ~ue to pollen, but a year-round affliction. My gratitude to . . . Spirulina ~oundless.

Salem, OR

From birth I have been plagued with numerous food allergies and hay fever. Since I have converted my diet to one of raw fruits, vegetables, nuts, herbs, and Spirulina, along with the cleansing fast, I am finally free of those physiological shackles. My yoga, meditation, and spiritual growth have been greatly enhanced.

Spokane, WA

I might mention that I was diagnosed a diabetic in December. Then started taking this [Spirulina] and exercising more. I've cut my daily insulin by 10 units now.

Spokane, WA

In March, 1981, I began taking [X brand] Spirulina tablets. Within a few days, I realized I had not taken my customary afternoon nap for several days. I seemed to have an increased amount of energy.

At about the same time, I had been diagnosed by my physician as being "pre-diabetic" and put on a diet of no sugars, white flour, etc., and also told to eat five smaller meals a day instead of three. I became concerned about two things. First, I was already about 10 lbs. overweight and was afraid the extra meals would add more weight. Secondly, I was concerned about my ability to resist the temptation of eating sweets and snacks.

I am really happy to say that within a month I had lost 6 lbs., had also lost my bloated feeling. Best of all, I no longer have uncontrollable cravings. I can eat one pretzel or one cookie, instead of the whole bag. I now eat a much more balanced diet and enjoy it more.

I can't say enough good things about [X brand] Spirulina. I not only have more energy but also a sense of well-being.

I have also stopped taking other vitamin supplements as I don't feel the need for them. I have cut the dosage in half of a diuretic tablet prescribed by my doctor many years ago. All in all, I really feel revitalized.

McMurray, PA

Personally we feel a great difference in our level of energy and in the level of concentration, not to mention a 70% improvement in a painful bursitis, through the taking of [. . .]*.

Mayer, MN

Severely allergic child returns to normal life

Roger Michaels† at age 5 years began developing a skin disease that caused incredible itching, swelling, and very dark circles around his eyes. Contact with poison oak meant an immediate rush to the hospital. Roger is now 13 years old. His life was not that of a healthy child, sleeping with blood stained sheets every night, not being able to participate in outdoor sports. A lifetime of doctor appointments, skin specialists, needles, skin grafts. He was allowed to go outside in the cool evening only, because doctors said he was allergic to the sun, to grass, to any kind of animals, even to his own sweat! His medications consisted of very harsh chemicals; they were loaded with cortisone. He was prescribed pills to control itching, which made him drowsy and fall asleep for hours in the afternoon.

As Roger grew up, his peers made fun of him, running away when he came by. The thing that was the hardest for me was the grown-ups stopping dead in their tracks to stare or to comment, "What happened to you?" At 13, Roger's skin had developed a very strange texture. It was always clammy, it was horrendous! He had open sores covering his whole body that seeped continuously, blood stains everywhere. His eyes had developed cataracts. But because Roger had spent most of his growing up years indoors, he had developed and excelled in academics. He now attends a special school for gifted children.

I had been taking Spirulina for about 6 months and it had changed my own patterns in my life, energy (very positive) and made the goals in my life much clearer. So when Roger came for the summer with a huge bag of drugs and creams, I couldn't let him do it any more. I sat down with him and said, "Let's do an experiment." I started with a Spirulina smoothie before I left for work and one when I got home. Also about 4–6 tabs a day, face mask [with Spirulina] every evening (worn all through the night) and [a Spirulina skin moisturizer] during the day.

Roger couldn't stand the taste of the smoothies at first, but by day 3 he actually liked it. He could even drink it [Spirulina] in ice cold water (but only if we were out of juice!)

---

† ...'s real name.

It took about two weeks to start seeing some results. But, I believed in what we were doing. So we persevered! Let me also mention that Roger was allowed his freedom! He swam down at the river, played with the dog, guinea pig and cat! Lots of sunshine. His clothes were always filthy when he came home, but he was enjoying!! Still those stares from grown-ups. I finally told Roger to ignore them and tell everyone he had poison oak; that would stop the curiosities.

The facial mask helped the itching so we began putting it on his arms and legs during the day. It started working very clearly after the first month. Roger was out every day. He even helped our dog when she was giving birth to five puppies. Now he's even exposed to more hairy animals.

He's got friends. The texture of his skin has changed. Do I dare to use the word, NORMAL? His personality has changed, open-hearted -- looks you in the eye -- *not down*! He is so happy, as happy as me, his mother. HE HASN'T READ ONE BOOK THIS SUMMER!

Boulder Creek, CA

From a mother with a handicapped child

Tony† was born with Hylane Membrane Disease, then as he progressed they called it BPD, Broncho-Pulmonary Dysplasia. Now it has been named Reactive Airway Disease. Basically all are new names for damage done by the oxygen and respirators. Tony has less than 50% of his lungs' capacity at the very best. Of course with any infection it drops considerably. As far as our doctors know, he is the oldest alive with his history and such severely damaged lungs. He has gone through all medical help here in Phoenix, Tucson, and was sent to Denver for experimental purposes. We decided he had earned the right to live or die at home, and have him still.

Tony has been on steroids since he was 3, and is steroid dependent. He has attended school about 2 yrs. total, of course, homebound teaching has been done. If he catches cold or an infection he must have the positive pressure machines, high doses of cortisone, theodur, terbutaline, and shots just to breathe. Of course oxygen is required too.

†Not his real name.

Since Tony has been on Spirulina he has had 2 colds, both of which he handled without increasing the drugs or using the machines, etc.! This is a wonderful miracle to us!! For unless we can get him off of the steroids he has little chance for much of a life!

Tony is 10 now, and about the size of a 7 yr. old. He is bright and happy (most of the time). He takes many more vitamins and healthful foods than drugs, even the research doctors had to admit he is much stronger physically than he "should" be.

Yesterday I was awakened by his coughing and choking. When I went to see, he was breathing very hard and asked for a treatment. I fixed a small amount of juice with a heaping teaspoon of Spirulina powder, along with it I gave him a theodur and terbutaline tablet. Usually when he is breathing that hard he will vomit anything given until he has an inhalation. Within 30 minutes, not enough time for the drugs, he was asleep, his breathing was labored but he rested. By morning his breathing was much better. No increase in the steroids, no machines, etc., and a hope for living -- this is what [. . .]* is giving Tony. It is truly an answer to prayer for us!

Tony takes a pound of powder every 3–4 weeks. If he is having a lot of trouble he requires more but generally not since Spirulina!

Morristown, AZ

Grandson was dying of cystic fibrosis

Our grandson at the age of 3 weeks was dying with all advanced symptoms of Cystic Fibrosis. [. . .]* and rebound exercise has kept it all under control (along with papaya enzyme). His symptoms were: very salty forehead, lethargy, all glands had shut down, he was not growing, mucus filled the lungs, very weak, gray pallor, no digestion so he was dying of malnutrition, stomach muscles weak, dehydrated and diarrhea. Now he is doing beautifully and everything is working.

Bellevue, WA

From a Viet Nam vet suffering from possible agent orange exposure

As a Viet Nam Veteran suffering from possible Agent Orange exposure (over the past 7 years) I've had great difficulty in digesting food. I've experienced just about all the symptoms of many of the metabolic disorders. Life has been a nightmare! My body has felt sore, stiff and achy constantly. Nausea is quite common.

For the past month I've been eating Spirulina. Peace, order, stability and strength have been returning to my body. There is a calmness within me which is much more life giving.

[. . .]* is proving to be an essential food in my healing. I will be eating Spirulina daily now.

Fairfax, CA

I was a victim of Agent Orange in Viet Nam and plagued by ill health for years. Since taking Spirulina in the last month I feel whole again.

So far the results are very impressive and I'd like other vets to know about it.

Berkeley, CA

Here are some of my beautiful experiences:

Blood pressure has been my major problem, especially when I get angry. My blood boils, I start feeling hot and shaky all over. I just reach for a bottle of [. . .]*, take two tablets and suddenly it subsides -- finally becoming normal.

And then, our *African hair*, it takes years to grow a good lengthy one, but what stimulus effect [. . .]* has on the hair growth, I'll really need to know why.

I used to be fond of potato chips very much. I could never turn away a plate of chips, no matter how full it was. But oh my! NOW I do not even want to look at them, no matter how delicious they smell. This has led to my weight being much better than ever before! Oh you should hear the compliments I get from friends and colleagues!

Nairobi, Kenya

I recently discovered [. . .]*. I have nothing but praise for it so far and a truly marvelous side effect has happened to me from taking it. My blood pressure has dropped markedly as a result of fasting with it and then just taking it prior to two meals, and in place of one meal each day. I cannot take hypertension drugs without bad side effects so I haven't taken any for a long time.

I am a mature woman of 53 and not prone to writing fan letters. But I am now. [. . .]* saved my life.

San Antonio, TX

Warm and cozy

For three days now I have been taking Spirulina. I am able to write this letter with some strength. My penmanship is returning -- I was an A-1.

I have had no other disease except high blood pressure. When it is "raging" 230/110 is normal and the pills I have to take make it worse until the dose is so strong (3 or 4 kinds) that I am "stiff." Might as well be an alcoholic!

The first dose (apple juice and Spirulina) hit my stomach hard. I thought I was going to have terrible cramps. But within 15 minutes it subsided and I felt "warm and cozy" like an infant after a bottle of warm milk.

Already I am taking only one pill (Ismelin) and 2 Apresoline -- all 10 mg's, about half my usual dose. I am afraid to tell my doctor but I feel good. No dizziness, no blurred eyes, no dry throat and no stiffness.

I have not felt so calm in my whole life.

It is very apropos that Spirulina has come at this time if it is the panacea of the world's woes.

Reseda, CA

It is exciting to see how much the Spirulina has helped my friends and especially what it is doing for my husband and myself.

Now, the reason for writing is this - I have a granddaughter 11 years old that has been recently diagnosed as having Neimann-Pick Disease. This is a very rare disorder which involves both a mental and physical deterioration of the body. When it was first suspected she had this, I put her on Spirulina, going from two [tablets] three times a day to five [tablets] three times a day now. In less than two weeks she became so much brighter and more alert. We felt she was physically better coordinated too. She had been stable at least for quite some time, but my daughter-in-law uses a chiropractor that has gone into some kind of practice treating people with many weird things. I was there once and couldn't believe what I saw him doing. He had told Nancy† to take her off Spirulina and told her to give her so many ounces of low-cal soft drinks and also so many ounces of chocolate with meals. He said her brain was starving for sugar. Cathy† immediately digressed.

. . . She is back on the regular Spirulina again . . .

P.S.   We are seeing wonderful results with [. . .]* on our friends with Leukemia.

Kennewick, WA

Skin cancer disappeared

I have been taking 100% Spirulina for about six weeks and I am taking it with a growing interest. My first interest in it was to try to lose weight. I can't say that I've lost much weight but I have lost inches and I am feeling better. I do not want to lose fast, as long as I am losing. My body feels good *and* my clothing feels good.

But let me tell you something I did not expect at all. I *had* a skin cancer on my right arm almost the size of a dime. It was active for a few days and again inactive for a few days. It was very red and I had fever in my arm. *Also* on top of my left hand *another* one . . . In a few days the redness and fever began to leave. In exactly two weeks these places had dried up, no scab or anything. These places continued to be tender for another two weeks — but after about six weeks, there is no sign at all. *Also* the small brown places on my hands are almost gone.

† Not their real names

I read everything I can get my hands on that is about this plant. I believe it is indeed a miracle plant.

Monroe, LA

I am depending on Spirulina powder to restore my health. Several months ago, after a visit to India, I got severe hepatitis and dysentery. This was also compounded by hypoglycemia, which I've had all my life. I lost over 40 lbs.

I . . . began eating only Spirulina and fresh fruit and juice. I was able to digest food for the first time in months. Now I am recovering my health.

Boston, MA

I am employed at a natural food store. Recently a woman came in, rather excitedly looking for Spirulina tablets or capsules. She claimed that her husband, while taking [. . .]*, had actually had a remission of his disease, multiple sclerosis. This greatly interests me because some years ago I was involved with helping folks with many different sicknesses and diseases and I felt (and still do feel) that M.S. is one of the worst health problems one can be stricken with. There are several levels of M.S. and I was working with the most extreme which was very heart-rending to me. I have a few friends with it who have slowly lost all use and control of their physical selves. As you may know, there is no known or at least medically documented cure.

I am somewhat convinced that some type of mega-algae program implemented in conjunction with a clean diet and other healthful practices, i.e. massage, acu, etc. would help these unfortunate victims of M.S. I firmly believe the time is now . . . for a rejuvenation of this planet's morale and values. A cure for multiple sclerosis by natural means using God's gifts may just help to open some now closed eyes.

Morro Bay, CA

Back pain is lessened

I have used about 3/4 of the [X brand] tablets and I am simply amazed at my response up to this point. I have been in constant, chronic pain since an automobile accident some 17+ years ago which damaged my spine in three places. The pain ranges anywhere from slight to severe and even with pain pills I still suffer a great deal, mainly from muscle spasm attacks which are apparently caused by chronic tension in my back and neck, due to being constantly in pain. Also it appears that I have an imbalance of the endocrine system.

The pain in my back injuries has lessened a great deal . . . so much so that it seems to be a miracle. I have greatly reduced my intake of pain pills. I do not feel nearly as much of the chronic tension in my neck and back and hence I am not having nearly as many muscle spasms. Also I am, generally speaking, feeling much better and it appears that my endocrine system may be righting itself. All in all, I feel as if I have stumbled onto a miracle! Even being able to type this letter (mistakes and all) is something I would not have been able to do prior to taking this Spirulina, for typing *always* brought on muscle spasms. I have recently typed a number of letters without muscle spasm attacks and only mild discomfort in my back injuries.
Winnemucca, NE

Our 5 year old contracted Spinal Meningitis when she was two. It took away her ability to walk, talk, self help skills, everything. Devastating. After years of healing with love, patience, and belief, she's walking and in school (Sp. Education). We started her on Spirulina in August and oh what improvements she's made. Gaining weight, she's sharper, clearer, and more and more healthy. We see miracles in my family through our experience with Tina † and I know when something is a gift from God to really make a difference and a contribution to all on a planetary level. Spirulina is it. I pray for the bringing together of all people and Spirulina.
Hana, HI

Infant almost lost to crib death

My son who is now 6 months old is alive today because of you. He was very sick at birth. He has pyloric stenosis, gastro-esophageal reflux and we have nearly lost him 4 times to crib death. When he was 3 weeks old, a friend told me to start giving him my plankton. I crushed them up and gave him 1 a day for a week. I noticed he was still the same but swallowing easier, so I decided to give him 2 a day. After 5 days he

† Not her real name.

was no longer choking to the point of suffocation and his color was more often normal than blue, as had been a pattern. Living in a small secluded town, I ran out of plankton and in 8 days he was back in I.C.U. with tubes everywhere. At this time we had no more money, so a friend gave me a bottle full. Within 4 days he was home, again in beautiful skin tone. Again we ran out and 7 days later he was back in I.C.U. with not much hope, and worse than before. I started plankton again and in 3 weeks he was fine again and home. They sent us home with an infant monitor and it sure sounds an alarm due to his "stopping spells" if we miss more than 2 days of 100% plankton.

I cannot get the doctors to agree with [X brand] as they are so "drug oriented" up here. They were going to turn me in for medical abuse because I refused to give my son their phenobarbital and other drugs. Finally after weeks of arguing they finally realized what he gets is just fine.

I am no genius but after almost losing my son four times to crib death I decided to do all the research and tests I could. After experimenting on my own son I honestly feel crib death is due to a Vitamin E deficiency. There are days we are all out of Spirulina and he goes very deep into sleeps and starts the blueness about the fingers and toes and lips. I start his "treatment" of Spirulina again and in 3–4–5 days he is normal again. I have timed his heart beat at 42 B.P.M. I give him 800 I.U. of Vitamin E and in one hour he is fine, back up to 100 again. If he is going through apnea spells I'll give him 2 crushed tabs daily of Spirulina, one at A.M., one at P.M. in a bottle of water or juice or cereal. Some days 2 or 3 times a month, I'll not give any at all just to let the protein level drop.

I really know very little about infant dosage but I do know it works at 2 tabs daily.

My son also (had) pyloric stenosis and gastroesophageal reflux. He seemed to spit up quite a bit but very seldom would he spit up Spirulina.

Even while I was pregnant I took Spirulina and boy did it help my morning sickness. If you ever hear of a near crib death case, I will be more than willing to answer any questions or just give relief in a much needed time. It is such a lonely feeling when your new baby is near death and you feel that every one is against your beliefs because you won't agree with their drugs.

My son is doing much better these days and I owe his life to you your wonderful time and effort into creating such an item.

DAILY SPIRULINA USAGE LOG SHEET
AND RECORDED RESPONSES

Aug. 9th we ran out of Spirulina and Aug. 16 we ran out of Vit. E.

AUG.

19	First apnea spell in 9 weeks - lasted 19 seconds.
21	Apnea spell lasted 22 seconds, heart dropped to 40 B.P.M.
26	Apnea spell, 69 seconds, needed to give mouth to mouth & C.P.R. for heart.
26	Baby was admitted in Good Sam Hospital for sleep study and E.E.G.
26	A.M. we received [. . .]* Spirulina and gave 1¼ tsp. dose.
27	Gave 1/4 tsp. at 6:00 a.m. - 12 p.m. - 6 p.m. - 12 a.m. for three days along with 800 I.U. of Vitamin E daily.
30	Color was back to normal - heart beat up to 120 B.P.M.
31	Apnea spell lasting 15 seconds but no discoloration.

SEPT.

2	Came home taking 1/4 tsp. Spirulina 2 times a day.
3	Heart beating normal - baby beginning to crawl again.
7	Baby still on 1/4 tsp. - 2 times daily. Vitamin E down to 400 I.U. per day.
10	Weighed baby - he had lost 2 lbs. but gained 1 lb. back.
13	Things seem to be going ok for baby.
14	Forgot Spirulina for 2 doses. Had heart drop to 52 B.P.M. in p.m.
14	5:00 p.m. gave 1/4 tsp. vitamin and 2,000 I.U. Vitamin E.
14	Was very tired today, no energy and didn't eat.
14	Nursed only 3 times in 24 hours. Drank 6 oz. water, 13 oz. juice.
15	Beginning to recognize Spirulina bottle - claps his hand and says "cooing" words. He actually loves this stuff. I find it to taste a little strong.
30	For the remaining month baby seemed pretty content. He is gaining now but the clinic says he is underweight. Birth weight: 9 lbs. 12½ oz.: 8 months: 16 lbs. 6 oz. But he looks good (good color).

Williams, AZ

NARCOLEPSY

Narcolepsy has a tetrad (4) of symptoms.
1. Sleep attacks
2. Cataplexy
3. Hypnogogic hallucinations
4. Sleep paralysis

Narcolepsy involves a nerve defect in the normal regulation of sleep and wakefulness. It is an overwhelming attack of sleep which the victim cannot inhibit, and which can occur several times a day. They experience extreme tiredness and fatigue for none of the normal reasons. The sleep attack relieves this, but only for a short period. Helpful is plenty of rest, no business or personal pressures. Drugs can have moderate to good control, but there is no effective and harmless treatment. Narcolepsy is the most dramatic of sleep disorders. It is chronic and the cause unknown. Age onset varies. From a study, 30% of the patients had an inheritance of narcolepsy and 10% go on to develop schizophrenic reactions.

Cataplexy is a sudden temporary loss of motor muscle control, brought on by fatigue and/or emotion. The typical cataplectic attack consists of a sudden dropping of eyelids, sagging of the jaw, slurring of speech, limpness of arms, then the knees buckle and the patient suddenly slumps to the floor. Once the condition begins, it usually continues over most of adult life. The patient is conscious during a cataleptic attack.

Hypnogogic Hallucinations

These are vivid auditory or visual illusions or hallucinations which occur while the patient is falling asleep. They usually occur in that state between wakefulness and sleep. They are so extraordinarily vivid and realistic that when the narcoleptic wakes up, he thinks he has had a real experience. Usually the hallucinations are frightening or terrifying.

Hypnopompic Hallucinations

These occur when the narcoleptic is coming out of a sleep attack.

Sleep Paralysis

This is a temporary paralysis of the cranial muscles and limbs. Sleep paralysis usually occurs in the interval between sleep and wakening, often on awakening in the morning or after a sleep attack. The narcoleptic awakens and finds himself completely unable to move.

Episodic Diplopia

This is double vision. Some narcoleptic patients experience this as a warning to an oncoming sleep attack or cataplectic attack.

Disturbed Nocturnal Sleep

The nocturnal sleep disruption is characterized by frequent awakenings during the night, although patients have no trouble falling asleep initially or following the arousals.

I have attempted a digested definition of narcolepsy, so the reader may have a better understanding of my testimony.

I was diagnosed as having narcolepsy in the early winter of 1971. I have experienced all the syndromes that are listed, the narcolepsy itself most of my waking hours; the cataplexy several times a day. There were at times one or two days out of the week that the cataplexy didn't seem to bother me. The hallucinations occurred several times a week. On rare occasion I had sleep paralysis. The double vision was a constant occurrence with the narcoleptic onsets. The disturbed nocturnal sleep was almost nightly.

For the first six years, I had acquired the intake of 120 mg. of ritalin per day. The first neurologist told me to take it as I needed it. Ritalin puts you on a real nervous, freaked out high. I would start with one 20 mg. spansule first in the morning. Then as I was coming down from the high, naturally I would take another. The problem is that, the periods in between the highs and lows would get shorter and shorter. I was literally a walking, working, extremely nervous zombie, with an uncontrolled temper.

In the fall of 1977, I was led to another neurologist and he was concerned at my taking ritalin and changed my medication to dexadrine spansules. He was also concerned with the amount I was taking, but he said if I needed it, I needed it; but for me to try and cut down. Through my unreasonable reasoning I felt I needed at least all of what I was taking just to get through my job and at home.

In the winter of 1978, I was led to another neurologist. He told me that if I took more than 20 mg. per day, there was a good chance I would be a permanent schizophrenic, and no matter what, there would come the day that I would have to quit working. Well I listened to him but I didn't heed what he told me.

I became a workaholic, and although I thought I was handling the situation just fine, there were often times, I just could not handle the smallest amount of any situation and periodically was suicidal.

I eventually did have to quit work and that was very devastating to me. I had no hope of ever leading a normal life. Because of my impossible personality, I became separated from my loved ones and was unable to keep my property financially and my world was falling apart.

It was toward the end of this devastating time, that I finally, finally, pleaded to God to take my life. It was then that He healed me by His divine power, from the drugs. Three years ago in August of 1979, I threw away all my medication and haven't taken any to this date. And I don't ever intend to take it again. There were no withdrawals. It was as if I had never been on the habit. I still had all the narcoleptic symptoms, but because of God I became spiritually aware of His wondrous healing spiritually, physically and mentally.

In August of 1982, God's Holy Spirit led me to a company that manufactures 100% Spirulina and other natural herbs and minerals. It was suggested to me that I try it. (Not for the reason of the narcolepsy, because they were unaware of my condition.) That day was the day that started my life to a normal active life. From the time that I started taking the 100% Spirulina and herbs I have not had any symptoms of the narcolepsy, cataplexy, hallucinations, double vision or sleep paralysis. It is as if I never had it. All that remains is the memories. This did not cure the narcolepsy because if I don't take the Spirulina and herbs, the narcolepsy and cataplexy, etc. does return.

All I know is, I feel healthy, with an alert mind and body. I praise and thank God for supplying the need for my welfare.

I pray that the medical society and all your readers that have narcolepsy, or if you know of anyone that does, that you seriously consider looking into what I have written down here. I truly believe this was not given for me alone, but for me to experience and to write down this truth for all that suffer from this disorder.

I pray also for God to bless you as He has blessed me.

San Jose, CA

Chapter 4

ENERGY UPLIFT

More energy to work with and play with, more energy to pursue the goals of success and a deeply fulfilling life is the common dream of many Americans who are just plain tired. Because Spirulina's special forms of protein and carbohydrates require relatively little energy to digest, it invigorates without the energy loss in digesting inefficient foods. The letters that follow describe the wonderful story of many a person's rediscovery of an energy-full life.

I've been fasting and using Spirulina and my body's never felt healthier. I've increased energy and clearer mind and I don't have the lethargic feeling I've been accustomed to with my normal diet. Spirulina has lived up to all the things I've read and heard and all my expectations.

Cheney, WA

I felt an intensification of my energy. Waking up without needing coffee. I especially notice that I don't experience my 4:00 slump in the afternoon. Weight loss, skin glowing. Feeling great!!

Boulder Creek, CA

I have much more constant energy, I need less sleep and my mind seems to be more alert, not so fatigued. My appetite decreased and weight was lost.

Boulder Creek, CA

I have taken Spirulina for approximately two months and have been exceedingly amazed at the energy I've experienced and the wonders of this natural food. It is indeed "imprisoned light."

Des Moines, IA

Dramatic increase in energy level

After 3 weeks using Spirulina I have noticed a dramatic increase in my energy level. I'm sleeping less. My body recovers incredibly faster from my runs. I'm running 30–40 miles a week with no problem. Before, I could only manage 20 miles and then I was constantly plagued by fatigue and mental dullness.

As far as I am concerned, Spirulina works! That's the final test of any product or service.

N. Hollywood, CA

A friend came down from an isle off Maine to visit, with jars of [. . .]* and even in the days of my wheatgrass and sprouts binges, never had I reached a plateau of such constant positive energy, good vibes and beneficence as from [these] tablets!

New York, NY

Executives at her company notice the difference!

About 3 weeks ago I read with interest an article in the "Enquirer" magazine on Spirulina. After reading the article like so many others -- I went down and picked up my first bottle of what would probably be a lifetime friend. Needless to say, this is the first time in my entire life (46) that I have beaten up the alarm clock and have more energy than I know what to do with. When I picked up my first bottle -- the stores were selling out -- I had to wait a week before I could get it but told a co-worker about it and shared my first bottle with her. She has lost a total of about 8 lbs. in those 3 weeks and is going through a lot of stress at this time and since taking Spirulina she has noted the same results that I have.

Another great thing that is happening -- executives at the company where I work have noticed my energy and have become interested in it -- today the president and Vice President/Engineering asked me where they could get it. Coming from them, that's a great compliment.

Edina, MN

We were introduced to [X brand] a year ago and love it! I always feel more alert, more energy and more functional when on [. . .]*, than with any other supplement combination.

Phoenix, AZ

I want to tell you how very much I appreciate the Spirulina. I have a lot more energy than I used to and I am able to cut back in my eating with it.

Franklin, PA

After trying Spirulina for the first time, four days ago, I was immediately affected by its outstanding qualities. I've been following a juice fast with Spirulina since then also. I've experienced a very positive "high" energy level both mentally and physically. This has also increased my spiritual harmony as well. I've been working and going to a health club all the while and I just ZOOM through the day; it's great.

Des Plaines, IL

A friend of mine recently introduced me to Spirulina and, I must say, I was immediately impressed by its invigorating properties.

Palo Alto, CA

From a psychologist . . .

I have been using Spirulina plankton for approximately two months. Spirulina plankton has been an enormous help to me. I have been a vegetarian (eating dairy products, but no meat, fish or eggs) for eleven years. About six years ago, probably because of my lack of attention to a balanced diet, I began suffering periods of fatigue. Various friends offered me help and advice, unfortunately some of them taking "fanatic" positions . . . telling me for example that I must be entirely macrobiotic or that I must eat nothing but fresh fruits or wheatgrass. I was, nonetheless, having trouble maintaining my busy schedule, and so I willingly tried going along with a number of programs. None of these attempts helped quite as much as does Spirulina plankton, which has genuinely impressed me. Since I began using it, my energy level has risen drastically (if somewhat erratically) and I feel much healthier and much more vital. I say that the increase in energy level has been erratic because I am still experiencing some periods of fatigue. These, however, are not long lasting and there is a general sense of improvement. Thus far, I have not attempted fasting; this I have avoided, again, because of my work schedule. . . . If I can take a retreat/vacation sometime soon, I will try some fasting. And whether or not that occurs, I will continue using the Spirulina, which is being sold in this area by five or six of my friends.

Let me add that I have also recommended Spirulina to one of my clients (I am a practicing psychologist). She is a 35 year old woman, 5'4" and 190 lbs., who has been seeking some healthy means of suppressing her appetite, and who reports some weight loss even after a short time.

I should have to note that fatigue was a very serious problem when I began taking [. . .]* -- and that it is the only program thus far that has helped me at all.

Let me hasten to add that I am deeply interested in the ways in which Spirulina could help the kinds of people who seek my help in counselling. There are several clients (over and above the one whom I have described) to whom I would like to recommend Spirulina. I am additionally interested in the fact that you are approaching issues in nutrition from a scientific standpoint.

Chelmsford, MA

I am so very happy with [X brand] Spirulina. I have taken it one week and here are the changes: deeper meditations, clearer mind, more energy. Sometimes I just stand and stare, the universe is so bright now, a week ago it was dull like my mind and now they are so wonderfully clear.

Layton, UT

Increased her workouts by 40%

[. . .]* increased my workouts by 40% and gave me a great burst of energy. I have never experienced this with any other supplement.

After having taught two 1-hour aerobics classes, I had enough energy to do a 2-hour nautilus workout. Spirulina is the best!

Soquel, CA

Until last November my hair on the top of my head had only been ¼–½" long for the last 15 years. Now it's grown an inch. I started taking [. . .]* tablets for the energy.

Arlington, TX

On the 12th of this month I tried Spirulina plankton for the first time. That morning in meditation I had the thought that I needed something for more energy as I had been "down" for the past six weeks and nothing seemed to do the trick. Later on that day, I tried my first teaspoon. I don't think I need to tell you what happened.

With the exception of one day I have been taking [Spirulina with bee pollen, ginseng and niacin]. The day I missed was, to say the least, very noticeable.

In addition to much greater energy, I've noticed greater concentration and even more importantly, a tremendous reduction of stress. So much so that it has been noticeable to many of those around me.

Phoenix, AZ

My sister gave me a bottle of [Spirulina with bee pollen and ginseng] tablets. I would like to know how I can purchase more. They are the best vitamins I have ever found. She has moved and we can't find anyone who knows where to get them. My bottle is getting low -- so please answer soon.

Corcoran, CA

I have been taking [. . .]* for the past two weeks and the results are extremely satisfying. The added energy, curbing of appetite and vitalizing feeling produced by this microalgae are incredible. I have encouraged many of my acquaintances to start taking it.

Alexandria, VA

Needless to say, we really appreciate the value of Spirulina, most especially [X brand] form. We had taken another brand before but did not realize any noticeable effects. The first time I did [X brand] Spirulina I was impressed enough to sign my name to a distributor agreement form. Within two weeks my wife felt the uplifting effects. Since then we have been spreading the news to anyone who will listen. We already have had many rewarding experiences. Both friends and relatives have realized some of the wonderful attributes of [X brand] Spirulina. Visualize the day when all people are benefitted by Spirulina!

Knoxville, TN

I fasted with Spirulina plankton for 36 days. My body cleansed itself of toxins, my thoughts became clearer and my heart opened up to the world around me. I had huge amounts of energy and if anyone had told me my whole life (mental, physical, spiritual and emotional) would change due to green powder, I would have told them they were crazy.

Boulder Creek, CA

"I could not get out of bed . . ."

I am taking 6–12 tablets a day and plan to start a fast when I can afford the fruits and vegetables. I am feeling so full of energy since beginning. I could not get out of bed it seemed, I had no energy. When I bought the powder -- I took 2 tsp. in carrot juice and went out and got a job. I have been going ever since -- taking 6–12 tablets a day.

Sulphur Springs, TX

I wanted to tell you I have been taking [X brand] 500 mg. tablets daily for the last week with my other vitamins and must admit I have noticed more energy even though I don't have a tendency towards lethargy.

Petaluma, CA

I am working for a chiropractor who carries Spirulina and have been using it for about 2 months as a dietary supplement. I have not as yet taken it upon myself to use it by fasting. I have noticed a marked improvement in my energy level since I began taking Spirulina and I am able to control my eating habits better when using Spirulina as an aid in losing weight.

Boulder Creek, CA

A friend introduced me to Spirulina. I have the [X brand] kind and credit it with my increase in energy and positive outlook on life. The Lord is the prime reason, of course, since He supplies all our needs!

Claremont, NH

Taking Spirulina is helping us keep strength through the day. We are very grateful for it. Quite a few at our community are taking it.

Pittsburgh, PA

Energy has increased drastically

I have been taking Spirulina plankton for about 5 weeks. Just this week I have noticed the change regarding my energy. It has increased drastically. Have started to lose inches but not pounds. Since I will soon be 53 years old I am just as happy with the inches because I feel the skin is firmer. My skin is moister and firmer, it appears lately. Also my bust is larger but my waist and hips are smaller.

Vallejo, CA

Chapter 5

IMPROVED HEALTH, PHYSICAL & MENTAL

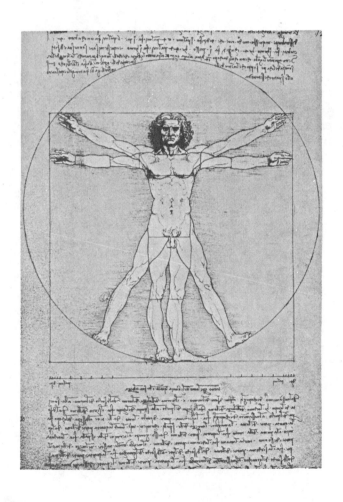

When our natural environment is being destroyed and contaminated substances injurious to our health are added to our foods, we must become aware of the relationship between nature and our health, and select the foods which are most natural, pure, and beneficial, and use them daily. Spirulina is such a food which can be used in a daily health program to give the individual the very best nutritional advantage. The letters that follow, indicating a wide variety of health improvements by individuals using Spirulina, attest to this fact.

I heard of Spirulina plankton in January 1981. I began using it in May, 1981. My, that was aeons ago! I used it consistently for 6 months and introduced it to my children and husband. Personally I was pleased with the increased energy and clarity of mind. I also noticed a change in my attitude. Prior to using plankton, I have been experimenting with vitamins, brewer's yeast, wheat germ, kelp, etc., different methods of cooking and preparation of whole fresh foods to add zest to my family's daily life. I also have specific concerns for two of my children. They have severe dairy product allergy and I've had to really search for foods to feed them to provide them with the balanced nutrients and to keep them breathing clearly and uncongested.

In order to put my observations about the effects of plankton to the test, I stopped using it for 6 months. There was definitely a difference in all of us. I began sleeping in - in the morning finding my head very groggy upon awakening. My young son turned into a real grouch and was difficult to talk to a good deal of time. My husband tends to be negative about our present economy, and became a really fearful, grouchy person recently, with the increasing pressure to find more work. He is a floorcovering installer and really appreciated the additional protein and energy from Spirulina plankton. My young daughter did not want to go to school sometimes and looked and acted lackluster.

June 9, 1982, we felt satisfied with the experiment and have resumed the use of Spirulina plankton. Each of us takes our Spirulina effortlessly; whereas before they took it because I wanted them to. They are convinced within themselves that this food is a necessary addition to their daily needs. Attitudes are at an all-time high in cooperation, lovingness, and family harmony.

Vancouver, WA

Her psychiatrist is mystified

I have taken anti-depressant and anxiety medicine for 12 years. Two months or more ago -- when I read the article about Spirulina in the National Enquirer, I started to take Spirulina. I don't know when it happened but I lost my anxiety and depression. My psychiatrist is delighted and mystified. He wanted literature on Spirulina, so I gave him that and 200-100% Spirulina tablets. He is slowly removing medicine from me. When I am off all of it, it will be a great victory for me and Spirulina.

[A friend] weighed 270 lbs. I ordered Spirulina for him. He lost 70 lbs. He had no choice. It was doctor's orders.

[He] coaches a youth football team. He is also a Boy Scout leader. He is into baseball in the summer time. He is so much more readily accepted by the youths' families, and also, by his co-workers. They want to know how he lost his weight. And he gets along with his co-workers better too.

Dad started taking Spirulina; about a week later he called me. He was so jubilant, he felt warmth in his lower legs for the 1st time in about forty years. He has always been a positive person anyway and felt pretty good. But he tells me now he feels like a 10 year old and from the energy he exudes I believe it. He says he'll probably live another 80 years now. You know, I wouldn't be surprised.

Mom started taking Spirulina the same time Dad did. She has diabetes and is a more pessimistic person than Dad. But a better mother never lived. I called one day and asked what she had been doing. She said, "I have been washing all day". She also said, "I couldn't do that before I started taking Spirulina." I said, "Mother, is it really helping you?" She said, "Yes." I couldn't believe my ears. She had been getting so feeble. It was music to my ears. She seems to have more life in her now.

Indianapolis, IN

From a teacher of dance and aerobics

I have followed [the] juice fast monthly for the past year and now with the Spirulina added to my diet I have physical and mental energy I've not had since my early twenties.

For the past eight years I was plagued with ulcers, gas, indigestion, canker sores, extreme abdominal swelling, very tender mouth and the list goes on.

At 25 years I had a hysterectomy due to this abdominal swelling. Now I can and probably could have controlled it with juice fast.

I endured 6 surgeries, all major, within 3 years. I never even after 6 years got any strength back, mentally as well. The quality of my life was very poor. Now I have more to offer not only myself but my family and others.

I now teach dance and aerobics and enjoy it.

Hollins, OK

Her doctor recommended Spirulina

I was advised several months ago by a doctor of internal medicine to start taking Spirulina. I went to a health food store and got a bottle of what they had in stock. I would be very interested in . . . selling this to my friends.

Three years ago I had surgery on the bottom of my foot that gave me a staph infection and left me with edema in the opposite leg. In the process, two hospitals were involved in my recovery. It will be a long process and much to my surprise after many tests I was sent to a health food store and advised to take Spirulina and another product that takes away fluid.

I feel I would be a good distributor for [Spirulina] since I do know a lot of people and many know how sick I was and how much better I look now.

Carlsbad, CA

Since I have used [. . .]*, I have experienced a great sense of health. It has given me a tremendous amount of energy, helped suppress my appetite, sped up sluggish metabolism and thyroid and helped me considerably with rheumatoid arthritis and iritis that had attacked my right eye. Being a vegetarian, I need the complete protein source of Spirulina and know that Spirulina is the most superior food available.

St. Louis Park, MO

In one week's time of taking Spirulina, my husband was like a different person, and the pain had left my gums. The dentist said I had periodontal disease and had me using salt water for months and it never helped at all. So we are sold on Spirulina.

Peoria, IL

I have been feeling better since taking [X brand] and after all my doctors, therapists, vitamin treatment, etc. I guess it's as close to a miracle that I'll ever get.

Richmond, CA

Father and brother admit they haven't felt so healthy in years

I've been using Spirulina for one year. During that time I have been healthier than for many years prior. Increased energy, shiny skin and hair, never even had a cold, while all around me last winter people had the Bangkok flu.

Furthermore, any time that I wish to diet I just do a Spirulina shake with some [Spirulina with bee pollen and ginseng, and Spirulina with niacin tablets] and my hunger diminishes. In fact, I have even more energy than usual. Many friends have had this experience but best of all my father and brother (both businessmen who love the good life - lots of food, wine, etc.) have been using it to diet and have really lost their appetites while admitting they haven't felt so healthy in 5 years. Also, their eating habits seem to have changed toward more live substances. It has meant a lot to me to be able to help my loved ones, family and friends in this way. It really feels that the quality of life is upleveled.

Cambridge, MA

I would like to share with you what [. . .]* has done for me.

My legs have been covered with red splotches for 8 to 9 years and I have been into the hospital twice with them. But now they are completely gone. They also left my daughter's legs. Also I had cysts in my breast—they are all gone too. My mother had blisters inside her mouth and throat that had been there for some time. I got her on Spirulina and now her throat is well and she has so much energy. My girl friend broke her leg and for 5 months she just sat. They put pins into it and the hole would not heal—it was the size of my thumb. The leg was swollen so large and they were planning on putting her back into the hospital and re-break it because it would not heal so I put her on Spirulina powder. In two week's time the wound was closed together, the swelling gone down. She threw away her crutch and is now walking everywhere she wants to go.

Garden Grove, CA

I have been taking 3 tablets of 100% plankton. I started with only 3 because I weigh only 100 lbs. and like to go slowly when I am experimenting. I am very happy to report that now that I'm in my 4th week,

I am still experiencing for the first time in my life (I am 36) clear nasal passages. I have tried many other diets, seen doctors, prayed and only Spirulina has helped.

Berkeley, CA

Lower back pain is gone

For 15 or 20 years I had a chronic low back pain that at times became so intense it completely crippled me and put me in bed. That too I had subjected to every known treatment, with no results. After four months on Spirulina - no more back pain.

Salem, OR

I have been taking Spirulina for a month and found it to be the answer to most of my problems, both mental and physical lethargy. Losing 12 lbs. was only a side bonus for me.

Cape Fair, MO

I have been using [X brand] only a short time, and so far the results of its effect on my system have made me feel better than I've felt in a long time.

Monterey Park, CA

A friend had brought a bottle of [X brand] Spirulina from California to her sister-in-law; she was so tired she could not work. She began to take them and she feels so much better. There are 6 or more [of us] who want them [now].

Elizabethtown, KY

I have been using Spirulina plankton for a week and have lost my craving for sugar - before, I used to crave sugar all the time - it's really like a minor miracle. I also feel stronger and more mentally alert.

Puyallup, WA

I just started taking [X brand] and I would like you to know that I can sleep better, feel better and I don't get junk food because it seems to fill me up and consequently I don't need it.

Detroit, MI

After my third fast with Spirulina plankton I noticed that it must be supplying my body with some missing nutrient. I am 16 years old, a vegetarian, and all my life I have had small white patches on my finger-nails. These white marks are quite common, I think. People told me that those white marks were Vitamin A deficiency, calcium deficiency, protein deficiency, and a trillion more deficiencies. However, after five days of fasting on Spirulina, they were almost completely gone.

Arlington, VA

Needless to say my wife and I know [X brand] Spirulina to be great stuff. We have taken it faithfully for the past few weeks, and we feel better generally than for several years. Something has put my gall-bladder and liver to work . . .

Scottsdale, AZ

Flu was over in 2 days. I continued eating the [Spirulina] soup for an additional day. It felt like it was helping me to detoxify quickly.

Boulder Creek, CA

Mental cobwebs gone

My boyfriend and I have been taking Spirulina for a couple of months. Within 2 weeks I felt a great difference. My mind doesn't even have the cobwebs it did before. My nails are growing, my nerves are calmer, and I don't get upset easily. Also I have a bad habit of not eating breakfast. I wouldn't eat lunch, except I got shaky, headache, and just felt generally bad. I take the Spirulina at breakfast, again at lunch time, and have had no more headaches, shaking, etc. I'm 30 years old.

Prescott, AZ

For the last four years I have been through therapy to release muscles bound by "psychological armoring." In the past, this release caused symptoms similar to having the flu, as toxins were released into my body. Since taking [X brand] Spirulina (for 1½ months) the flu-like symptoms have disappeared, my body is able to cleanse itself without depleting my energy. Also, the therapy is moving faster now that I can physically handle more changes.

[. . .]* has also cut my appetite. I no longer have a desire to eat between meals, and only feel the need of two meals a day.

I am 36 and work out at a gym five days a week, and work. Since Spirulina I can feel the difference.

Jacksonville, FL

[Results using (. . .)* are] increase in energy, mental clarity and "brightness". The most extraordinary result is the effect on intestinal elimination. As a result, the effectiveness of my elimination has improved 200%–300%.

Boulder Creek, CA

Recently I have been fasting and taking [X brand Spirulina with comfrey and pepsin]. I have not felt as healthy in years. . . . My roommate is a distributor and I have heard many impressive testimonies even from one woman who had been classified previously as handicapped and gets around great today.

Northfield, IL

A friend sent me a bottle of [X brand] Spirulina from Seattle. She has been taking it for about 6 months. It has changed her life and [I] can understand why! During the time I took [X brand] Spirulina, my mood was better, my energy level was increased, my body felt healthy and my bad vision at night started to get better!

Missoula, MT

I am on a nutritional program, which I discontinued in October to go on a Spirulina fast. I have been feeling better. I get a massage every week and my skin texture has definitely improved since I have stopped my nutritional program and stayed on [the] fast.

Parkville, MO

Heartburn decreases

I am very enthusiastic about Spirulina. I have been taking it for about six weeks. I was bothered terribly with severe heartburn due to a bad hiatal hernia. Since taking the Spirulina I have not had to use any antacids, for which I am very grateful.

Lakeside, OR

Last April (1981) while in Salt Lake City, Utah, my brother, a dentist, told me about Spirulina because he knew my body did not properly assimilate protein. I became a distributor in order to purchase [Spirulina] wholesale for my own use.

I have been taking Spirulina since that time and can honestly say, I've never felt better. Also I have lost 18 lbs. without dieting. I feel that because my body is getting the nutrition it needs, my appetite has sharply decreased. My weight loss has been slow but steady and I also feel I will not regain the weight.

I seldom eat sweets as I used to do and they even taste undesirable to me when I do.

I am proud to be a part of the . . . Family and will never quit using [X brand] myself.

Pocatello, ID

Goes up and down stairs like a whizz

I sure like [. . .]*; it's done so much for me, especially my breathing power. I take only 1 breathing pill a day, used to need them every 3–4 hours. Can go up and down stairs again like a whizz (a 53 year old whizz). Don't sleep much any more. Used to sleep, sleep, sleep. I even mailed three bottles back to California this week to my mother and brothers.

Delano, MO

A few comments from a friend after using Spirulina powder for a week. This is after several years of extreme difficulty with food allergies.

She had hunger pangs after not having any appetite for years. Inner trembling calmed. Depression lifted. Better bowel movements. More energy. Thinking a little sharper. Memory a little better. Hard feeling in stomach relieved.

Lafayette Hill, PA

Do you know what? - I can't believe *me* is *me*, because of the added strength, energy and well-being that is mine since Spirulina became a part of my regular food! It seems like a miracle!

Mission, TX

Migraines disappear

Since the age of 16, I have experienced clusters of debilitating migraine headaches. On Dec. 31st, 1981, I took my first Spirulina tablet. I have been taking 15 to 20 tablets daily of 5 different formulas. I have not had one migraine headache since Dec. 31, 1981. In addition, my energy level has been raised to a point where I no longer have to take a nap in the afternoon which had been my previous pattern throughout the years.

Rancho Palos Verdes, CA

Six months ago I started the Spirulina program. I had Phlebitis in my left leg with a black spot the size of one's hand. Since then, the black spot is thinning out and steadily disappearing. The huge swelling in my leg has totally disappeared. I have lost 25 lbs. and my doctor is amazed at the way I look and feel. I have much more energy and am able to do things I could not do before taking Spirulina.

Redondo Beach, CA

I had an alcoholic problem for 5 years or more. I was in a deep depression and at a physical low in my life. I felt a desperation words can't describe. I felt life was over and all I had left was a living hell. This I couldn't cope with. (I had always loved life.) My friend told me about Spirulina many months before I reached the lowest point in my life. I thought "Oh yes" but not for me. One Sat. in Sept. 1982 I called and asked for help—I needed help—I started on [Spirulina with comfrey and pepsin], [Spirulina with Vitamin C, papaya and cayenne], [Spirulina with trace minerals] and [100% Spirulina] that day! My desire to drink, or any craving for liquor seemed to leave and my mental state began to improve almost immediately, each day became more alive and an inner peace seemed to take over. I have not had or wanted a drink for 2 months. Yes there is life without alcohol. I truly believe Spirulina was the answer. I have also lost 15 lbs. with no effort.

Rancho Palos Verdes, CA

Our daughter who is diabetic has had much pain in her feet and legs until she could not sleep nights, and at this point, anything is worth a try. She began to take these pills three times a day in large amounts and has had much, much relief for which I praise God, our Creator who giveth man the wisdom to discover His great Creation.

No. 2. I have a man, our neighbor, who is a farmer and rancher, doing lots of leg work. He tried one bottle and came back and bought more and has asked I save him another one. Since he has taken this Spirulina, he has not taken one aspirin whereas before, he lived on them. He is very satisfied and helped.

No. 3. I also have a young mother who has had headaches constantly and since taking Spirulina, she told me, her headaches are gone (and she lost a few pounds).

I think the good this Spirulina has done, outweighs the darkness spread around. I take this Spirulina and am much helped. Can do a good day's work at the plant where I work and also work at home, besides all the extras. Several ladies are taking this as well as men where I work and can vouch for the help in energy and the lift to help through our busy, busy days.

We'll come out as winners because the truth always is a winner. May take time, but the truth always prevails.

Ontario, OR

From a recovering alcoholic

I am a recovering alcoholic woman with 2 years of sobriety. Four months ago I started taking Spirulina Plankton tablets and also the powder. I take 7–10 a day.

The clarity of my main goal (sobriety) has been enhanced ten-fold. Alcoholics tend to be very negative people - result - drunk. Spirulina has *balanced* my physical being as well as my mental being (i.e. less confusion felt, willingness deep inside to maintain my goal, more open-mindedness, a strong desire to live).

Spirulina is a definitely beneficial help to me in my sobriety because it equals balance, which I have never known in my lifetime before because of my self-destructive path.

For any alcoholic (drinking or sober) I *heartily* recommend Spirulina as a part of your life. Sobriety and Spirulina allowed my true spirit to emerge for which I will be eternally grateful.

Bonny Doon, CA

Waking up from the nightmare

In January of 1982 I had, so they say, "hit the bottom." Through one solid year of caffein, cigarettes and over-the-counter diet aids, I had developed into a full-fledged hypoglycemic. That wasn't the worst of it; instead of going for natural sugar in protein, I went for the processed sugar in alcohol.

Waking up popping the diet pills, followed by a pot of coffee and at least half a pack of cigarettes was all to get me going and on the road to accomplish something. Around three in the afternoon, I would take another pill to assure a productive evening. By nine p.m. I would be ready to wind down and try to rest, but by that time I was so wired I couldn't relax, so I would buy a six-pack and drink until I almost passed out.

This nightmare went on for a full year until one day I heard about Spirulina on TV. That night I bought a bottle of plankton and almost immediately after consumption I felt a natural energy boost. Making the decision not to take the diet pills was very easy because my appetite was supressed and I had plenty of energy from the [. . .]*.

Giving up the alcohol was something I was unable to do. I tried and tried and eventually brought myself to admit that my body was no longer craving the sugar, so there had to be something wrong with me.

February 26, 1982, after a very self-destructive drunk, I finally reached out for help and have not touched alcohol since that time.

In a sense, I feel that Spirulina plankton has saved my life! Without the physical healing the [X brand] products provided for me, I would never have admitted to a mental and spiritual healing.

Through the use of Spirulina and the Grace of God, I am finally on the road to a healthy, happy and holy way of life.

Dallas, TX

Help for poison oak

Spirulina has changed my life in a way that will never be changed back again. Whenever I really need to be on the ball, I take 12 [. . .]* and know that my energy level will remain high for many hours and the "sleepies" won't interfere with my concentration and alertness. I excel at my job and I put a lot of energy into it and so the boost that Spirulina gives me at the times I really need it, and the boost it gives to my overall health is a treasure that I will not be without. The treasure of good health! I have Spirulina to thank more than any other food or supplement or diet regime I've been on in my life. I thank God for the marvel of this miracle food. I'm grateful for the opportunity Spirulina has made for my life in business. Words stop here as my feelings go on flowing.

I have an interesting story to tell you. I've taken Spirulina for years. Recently, I've found a new application. Yearly, I go through a bout with poison oak which I get from my cats. This year I had a worse case than usual. I've long taken [Spirulina with niacin, calcium gluconate and B-6] before Jazzercise - it helps me have an excellent work-out. I'd take [it] and my poison oak would itch like crazy. Lucky I had the Jazzercise to occupy me. Then I'd go home and put the face mask (with Spirulina) on the outbreak. My poison oak began to heal very quickly. I thought it was all due to the face mask. But now I'm not so sure. I believe the niacin in the [tablets] opened up the capillaries (as in the Niacin flush) and helped cleanse the rash which is on the surface of the skin. Those two products in combination ended my poison oak much sooner than it usually takes me to overcome it.

Boulder Creek, CA

I have been using it now for over a week and am experiencing the most marvelous effects of this miracle food. For the past three years I have been seriously sick but have had to work every day—and you can imagine the wonderful change that has come over me. I am like a new person. It has seemed like a miracle that I have been able to find this gift.

Binghamton, NY

Chapter 6

FASTING
COMES EASY

A few years ago, fasting was either a practice followed only by Biblical characters or by modern health food fanatics. But today, many people in every walk of life are discovering the wonderful benefits of giving their internal organs a rest from the digestion process, and giving the body a chance to "clean out." Because Spirulina provides excellent nutrition and in powdered form can be mixed easily with fruit or vegetable juices, it has proven an excellent basic ingredient to the fast. The faster can give up solid food for days, losing weight without feeling low-energy or even hungry.

Nothing but positive results

My doctor, a chiropractor-wholistic physician, advised me for health reasons to begin fasting. I hesitated for the right time, knowing then that I could handle a 5–7 day juice fast, but not really excited about it. In the meantime, I began using Spirulina as an addition to my diet. The results were excellent. Most obvious, clarity of mind and added energy. My doctor and I agreed, Spirulina would be an answer to my fast.

June 13, 1981, I began a 2 week fast using juice, Spirulina [X brand], cleansing herbs and water. The first day went well with little hunger. Day 2, I ate an apple along with the others to help clean the digestive system. Hunger followed. I began enemas using 1 teaspoon Spirulina, 2 teaspoons glycerine and 1½ quarts distilled water. Because I had experienced much auto-intoxication as part of my ill health, I continued daily with enemas. After 10 days of easy fasting, I continued on to 15, then 22, on to 28.

My fast lasted 38 days. I was under constant supervision and saw nothing but positive results. They correspond to other reports of similar fasts I have read.
 1. Pink, strong nails
 2. Shining, soft hair
 3. Supple skin
 4. Weight loss 116–103
 5. More constant positive state of mind. Able to handle stress better.
 6. Clearer thinking
 7. Less sleep
 8. Higher physical energy level
 9. Improved meditation
10. Not to mention the internal cleansing and changes.

An average daily routine: 1. Shivambu Kalpa upon rising. 2. One teaspoon [X brand] Spirulina four times daily. 3. 3–4 quarts distilled water daily. 4. Daily enema for 25 days, then every 2–3 days.

Also on the positive side, which didn't seem so at the time, is the emotional dumping (cleaning house) and physical cleansing (bad breath, coated tongue, body odor).

I have nothing but praise for [X brand] Spirulina and fully believe it is food sent from God.

Tucson, AZ

I am very interested in your Spirulina plankton - very impressed. I feel as though I have finally found "it" in the world of diet and nutrition.

I haven't felt able to fast for months and months due to having experienced far too much irritability and weakness on attempted ones, but there's no problem on this one with Spirulina. The purification process is also incredible.

Los Angeles, CA

I had a Spirulina Booth at the Cancer Control Convention in Los Angeles, July 3–5, 1981.

I met a man named Michael that at that time had fasted on [X brand] Spirulina for 56 days and intended to go for 60. He looked great and said he felt good.

Reseda, CA

51-year old teacher feels great

I commenced the 7-day fast/enema program. I was careful to follow [the] instructions, and I also included the lemon juice/maple syrup routine.

The results were close to magical. What seemed like years and years of waste and junk were expelled. I could almost put my finger on the time era of my life when energy and enthusiasm were about "equal". As I am now 51 years of age, I determined the peak "health years" were those spent in a small town college dormitory. During [the] Spirulina fast, I was cleaning house like crazy, into four mile hikes, and giving three times the preparation to my teaching preparation (assignments). Remarkably, my complexion took on a youthful dewy look, and I was more patient and relaxed with students and aides.

I discovered I could no longer keep nightowl hours, and had to "turn in" by 11 PM as I did during my college years. I was glad to do so, however, and discovered the rest I previously had gone without.

One of the most remarkable occurrences was a sudden return to the menstrual period. The "heat waves" I had been experiencing for a number of months subsided, and my body temperature seemed "cooler."

Wauchula, FL

I have had a health food store for more than 20 years, and have now retired. Now I do a small business from my home with products I have found to be special.

Spirulina seems to be a very special product.

I am on my first Spirulina fast, after many others through the years. Only you and yours would believe the difference!

Walking very tall!!

Dayton, OH

I have recently discovered the joys of Spirulina and will continue to use it for the rest of my life. Fasting is really easy with [. . .]* and when I am fasting it gives me wonderful energy, not to mention glowing skin and all that stuff.

Los Angeles, CA

Doesn't feel hungry

I have been fasting with Spirulina plankton for 8 days now. I haven't had the desire for food for about 5 days. I'm really impressed with the results of this wonderful algae. I have gotten my sister started on it. She loves it. Thanks for discovering it in my lifetime. I have always been a compulsive eater and tried everything to lose. I'm losing now and not feeling hungry and don't feel like eating compulsively.

Sacramento, CA

I fast one week out of each month, and one day out of each week. I lost ten pounds the first full week's fast and felt no hunger pangs more severe than during a usual day of eating three meals. I fasted exactly according to [the] instructions on fasting with Spirulina, and experienced much more energy, zest for life and feeling of well-being. Many of my aches and pains left me. During my one day fasts, I feel much more vigorous and notice a return to lack of this vigor when I spend the day eating.

Fullerton, CA

I've been fasting for 21 days and never felt better. I am interested in receiving any and all information you may have about this incredible food!

Burlingame, CA

A 30-day fast at the Grand Canyon

Would like to do a 30, or so, day fast up here at the Grand Canyon. Last year we did a 30 day fast. The results were excellent. Daily elimination during the fast was remarkable and we felt keen and strong during the entire 30 days, with the exception of a couple of days near the end when we were slightly weak. I've done water fasts up to 40 days about seven years ago and the results of the Spirulina fast were much better. We felt like we were being nourished and repaired while fasting and our energy level was unusually high.

Tusayan, AZ

I first had Spirulina last summer when I lived in Phoenix, AZ. It was a blessing. When it's 115° and you don't really like eating anyway, you can find yourself in a predicament. Spirulina saved me. I didn't fast properly and now that I know how, I will! During that time I lost 20 lbs. and never realized that I was getting down to where I longed to be. So I was able to have my "cake and eat it too." I'll write again to let you know how I'm doing.

May the Force Be With You.

New Carlisle, OH

I am a user of the blessed Spirulina and am convinced of its magic powers. I am presently on a fast with Spirulina and it's so pleasant, easy and satisfying!!

Makawao, HI

I am at this moment in Day 13 of my own juice fast with the use of Spirulina and can't tell you how thrilled I am.

I am a novice herbalist and beginning to just scratch the surface of the many good things people should be educated about in order to acquire good health. But I am truly excited about this algae which has given me more energy than I have had in many a month.

Hollywood, FL

I went on my first fast . . . and felt absolutely wonderful! (even though toxins were *pouring* out of my body!). Now I supplement my raw diet of sprouts, fruits, and vegetables with Spirulina.

Santo Domingo,
Dominican Republic

I am presently on a Spirulina fast and I feel terrific on the 4th day. I plan to continue for a week to rid myself of toxins and hopefully of the migraine headaches I have been suffering from for 3 months. Actually, the headaches are subsiding.

Whistler, B.C. Canada

107-day fast—"I felt totally rejuvenated"

I've suffered with a few chronic physical ailments for as long as I can remember. I've had multiple allergies, sinus problems, chronic acne, itchy scalp with excessive dandruff, and hypoglycemia. In the past few years I've learned that these are all signs of excessive toxicity of the body, particularly involving an unhealthy condition of the intestines. I've refined my diet and fasted occasionally, but these toxic signs have always remained. When I heard that [. . .]* contains a wide range of nutrients as well as helps eliminate toxins from the body, it sounded like a great way to go on an extended fast and get my body healthy once and for all.

I lived for 107 days on a fasting diet with Spirulina plankton, as recommended in the book *Rejuvenating the Body through Fasting with Spirulina Plankton*. For the first 30 days I consumed one to two teaspoons of Spirulina per day with vegetable broth at lunch and I drank fruit juices in place of the other regular meals. For the next 64 days I consumed between one to three tablespoons per day of Spirulina with liquids. This makes a total period of 94 days during which I ate nothing more than Spirulina plankton and liquids. For another 13 days following, I ate Spirulina in vegetable broth at lunchtime and I had solid juicy fruits during the other mealtimes. I ingested the Spirulina in the form of a broth made also with tomato juice, distilled water, one tablespoon miso, a pinch of dulse or kelp powder and a pinch of cayenne and ginger powder. The total liquid intake amounted to approximately two to four quarts a day. I also ingested two to six [. . .]* daily to help speed toxic elimination. I had gone through a few intensive healing crises with fever, heavy mucus elimination and tiredness during the first three weeks; these grew shorter and less intense as the fast proceeded. I am one of those people who stay at a constant, slightly underweight state and only lost four or five pounds during the fast. I have always been underweight even though I have done a lot of overeating. My body seems to require a certain moderate amount of nutrition and the habitual eating of large amounts of heavy foods for the past several years had overburdened the digestive system and caused this state of toxemia. During the fast, my tongue slowly got clear of the thick whitish coating that had covered it during the fast and in the mornings upon awakening. This is a sign that the colon is cleaning up. A red layer appeared below the white tipped layer of my fingernails, which is a sign of improved circulation. I have also been able to breathe more deeply and clearly than I have been able to for years. My daily yoga and meditation have greatly improved due to better breathing and circulation. By the end of the third week I had lots of energy and maintained a vigorous and healthy state for the rest of the fast. At the end of the 107 day period, I gradually started to eat sprouts and salad vegetables and I am now eating grains and cooked vegetables as well. I feel I get much more nutrition from the food I eat now due to a healthier intestinal tract.

I also feel overall much more in tune with my body due to this fast. The nutritional and cleansing properties of [. . .]* enabled me to continue on the fast for the period of time my body really needed in cleansing of toxins. The allergies and "tired feeling" that had bothered me chronically during my past vanished completely during the fast and by the end of the 107 days I felt totally rejuvenated. I couldn't have done it without [. . .]*.

Boulder Creek, CA

Dieting without doctors, pills, or clubs

I'm on my 6th week of successful dieting without the support of doctors, pills, clubs or any organization boosting my will power and I am very enthusiastic about the way I feel and attribute it directly to plankton.

Rainier, OR

I bought some Spirulina plankton from a friend. I have been fasting for eight days, today. I have never taken anything like this before. I have chronic bronchitis but since I started on this amazing tablet I feel so much better in this short time. I would like to read more about this.

Orangeburg, SC

I have been taking Spirulina plankton for about two weeks. The first week, I took Spirulina to help cut my bad eating habits down. So I took it and continued to eat, but not as much. Then I went to a health food store to find a book about Spirulina, read it and started fasting the second week, with Spirulina and fruit and vegetable juices. I feel like a new person in many ways, plus I have tried many ways to lose weight and now I think Spirulina will help me. Please give me more pointers on dieting with Spirulina.

New Orleans, LA

In January [1981] I went on a seven day fast - not my first, but my third in a three year period. The only difference between this fast and the others was that I used Spirulina exclusively this time. The differences were incredible - first, I felt absolutely no craving for food. The [. . .]* seemed to control my appetite to the point where I felt no urge to eat solid foods. Secondly, I had more energy than I ever had before while fasting. I did all my normal household activities, went hiking, and even felt energized enough to run each day in addition to my usual yogic exercises. Lastly, I had a wonderful sense of calm and patience while dealing with my little girl and other stressful situations at that time. Most people become irritable and short-tempered while fasting and I am sure the Spirulina prevented this from occurring as it was the only different thing I did between this fast and the others.

Since that time in January, I have done several one day and a three day fast. The same sense of energy-filled well-being and lightness accompanied these fasts. I become very clearheaded during these times - it seems as if my brain cells become "super charged."

Finally, I have to add that my problem with cold feet seems to have diminished with the intake of [. . .]*. I find that I can withstand cooler temperatures without having to pile on so much clothing. I suspect therefore that it has begun to improve my circulation.

So, based upon my personal experiences, I would like to confirm to you that [. . .]* has been a beneficial appetite suppressor when fasting, it produces feelings of well-being in times of stress, it also assists in lucid thinking, it gives the body a tremendous amount of added energy, it helps with problems of the underweight (perhaps by balancing the metabolic rate), and it improves circulation.

I am *very pleased* with the effect this miraculous food has had upon my life. Of course, I will continue to use it and make as many folks as possible aware of its benefits.

Silver City, NM

I've been fasting and feeling good on Spirulina. I have much weight to lose and plan on continuing the fast for several months. I am keeping a journal of this experience and would like to keep in touch with you about all this. I need to lose 150 lbs. altogether and feel that I can do it with Spirulina.

Toronto, Ont., Canada

He has never felt better than on this fast

I would like to report that I have just completed eight days of fasting with Spirulina plankton, in strict accordance with instructions in *Rejuvenating the Body Through Fasting with Spirulina Plankton* and very honestly have never felt better.

After the third day, mental energy was up substantially. I experienced greater mental alertness, the need for less sleep, and meditation was significantly improved. My physical energy was down until the fifth day, at which point it rapidly caught up to the feeling of euphoria I was experiencing mentally. My body has never felt purer. On the seventh day I visited the health club that I belong to and lifted greater weights for longer periods than I am accustomed to, and felt better doing it.

Chicago, IL

My wife has lost 20 lbs by . . . Spirulina fasting and her moods have become very positive. We are very thankful.

Sacramento, CA

I fasted for seven days and was never tired or sick or hungry. I couldn't believe it. This was in October. I am now on the maple syrup, lemon juice program to lose 5 lbs. I am 67.

Grand Rapids, MI

My wife and I tried fasting as prescribed in [the book] *Rejuvenating the Body*, and it has certainly worked for us. We thought that fasting would cause us to feel exhausted and hungry but as the week progressed we lost weight, felt lighter and better than ever before.

Spirulina is truly a wonder food and we have changed our perspective concerning diet and good health. Now my spouse and I try to fast once every two months but pure Spirulina is difficult to find in this area.

Chattanooga, TN

I have the book *Rejuvenating the Body through Fasting with Spirulina Plankton*. The first time I fasted using Spirulina and fruit juices, it affected my mind so much I could not believe it . . . as if I was high, I guess. And where did all the energy come from -- unbelievable!

Hamtramck, MI

I did a 30 day fast -- the last 15 days of that I had a couple of raw meals. I was taking fruit juices with Spirulina and bee pollen with a few vitamins and Vitamin C. I must disagree that enemas are not necessary! You must get the poisons out of your system to rejuvenate! I had colonics and was taking "sea cleanse" with my juice to form bulk to push through the digestive canal. I eliminated some heavy "junk". I had weekly colonics. I also took Bentonite and several herbs for tissue cleansing. I felt energetic at first and then the toxin elimination got so heavy it was making me tired. However, I was getting proper nutrition, I know, because my work is very strenuous (I exercise race horses at the So. Calif. racetracks) and I suffered no loss in strength. I am continuing periodic fasting with fruit juice, herbs, etc., enemas, colonics, and am taking the Spirulina, bee pollen, and vitamins continuously.

Bonsall, CA

And what a light Spirulina is above the darkness! The rays of the light force attain to enlighten all of humanity. I recently fasted for fourteen days using [Spirulina with comfrey and pepsin] tablets, juices, and ginseng tea. The effects of meditation and chanting were more pronounced during this fast and I am enjoying the benefits of perfect digestion.

Cincinnati, OH

Feels physical and spiritual well-being during fast

I am distributing the Spirulina here in N. Carolina. I fasted for 7 days on it and saw remarkable results in my physical and spiritual well-being.

All in all I'm in perfect health and since the fast my eyes have cleared considerably, I'm no longer constipated ever, and I have not had a herpes simplex outbreak (this is the most remarkable thing, as I was averaging one every two weeks.) This may be in part due to a considerably lessened sex-drive. (The herpes were on my genitals). Also my physiological well-being has improved and I have stopped actively using marijuana after 10 years. I also dropped my weight by about 15 lbs. and for the first time in my life really feel comfortable with my body. My posture has improved also. All in all, I'm quite excited about this food and see it not as "Just another Fad" but as something so much greater. I've convinced some other people to try the fast and their experiences have been extremely good.

Edneyville, NC

I am very pleased with results, as it does indeed have the effect of curbing my appetite, allowing me to concentrate on my programmed diet. While it tastes perfectly horrible, I am not about to give it up; as awful as it tastes, it's not nearly as bad as fighting to keep away from overeating.

Fresno, CA

Fasting has been "quite easy"

I'm in the ninth day of a fast, Spirulina, that is.

My fast has been going quite nicely. I take two tsp. of Spirulina powder each meal and a couple of tablets, either two [Spirulina with niacin tablets or a Spirulina with niacin and Spirulina with bee pollen and ginseng tablet] when I feel weak or tired. After the first two days, it's been quite easy. I really haven't had a hunger pain in days, and I'm actually getting to like my Spirulina drinks.

Most importantly, the allergy symptoms have all but disappeared. When they finally go, which I expect in the next two or three days, I'll end my fast. Over all, it has been quite easy.

Minneapolis, MN

After spending only a four day fast upon plankton, I was able to work hard and continue round the clock on only a few hours sleep without any body tensions or feelings of tiredness. Completely remarkable new experience for me. Didn't really expect any results after such a short period of time.

London, England

I would like to let you know, my experience with [. . .]* is that it is an excellent appetite suppressor. I fasted on it for 12 days, working full time as a carpenter and had no weakness or hunger. My wife is a teacher aide and fasted on it for 20 days with the same results.

Redwood Valley, CA

I have personally lost 20 lbs in 5 weeks eating [X brand] Spirulina. I am hypoglycemic and have never been able to fast until I began eating Spirulina. I fasted four days successfully. I feel energy like I have never felt before. I also find I have a clear mind and a better memory. I tried going without Spirulina for two days and I really lost my energy. I believe in this food and I know it works. Nothing else gives me energy like [. . .]*. I pray our F.D.A. will let this food continue to be sold in the U.S.A., for I've never known a nation of more overstuffed yet undernourished people.

Fairfield, CA

My introduction to Spirulina was made while I was searching the best mode of fasting in New York City. I began my fast and have been going very strong (now in my 8th day) so far. My high activity (my own business, Karate and study of music) has only been enhanced by the Spirulina, and my slight skin impurities are being cleansed by [. . .]*.

New York, NY

Loses weight impossible to lose before

I have used [Spirulina] myself with fantastic results while fasting. I began to lose weight that was impossible to remove before.

Evansville, IN

From a competitive runner: racing improved during a fast

I have been a competitive runner on the Woodside Strider running club for twelve years and have tried all kinds of foods and supplements but Spirulina by far has been the most effective. It's the only thing I have found that has given me what I was looking for: an energy boost. I could drink it while in a long race and feel a real lift in my energy. Ever since I have used Spirulina my racing has really improved. Last month while on a three day fast using Spirulina, I ran my best race ever, out of five hundred and sixty runners I came in twenty-first and that was on my third day of the Spirulina fast. I am looking forward to longer Spirulina fasts and better racing.

Boulder Creek, CA

I want you to know how my husband and I enjoyed and renewed our health with Spirulina plankton. We had planned to go on a water extract fast, which we did, but while on the fast we became acquainted with Spirulina through our Natural Doctor. We went to have an iridology reading and the doctor acquainted us with Spirulina.

The water extract fast consists of using 6 ounces of diced carrots, 4 ounces of diced beets and 2 ounces of diced celery, placed in a 1/2 gallon of distilled water and let sit overnight. In the morning you drain the fluid off and throw away the vegetables. You drink the entire amount of fluid daily. The first two days one drinks only the extract, but on the third day one can add a teaspoon of honey to each glass of extract. When we learned of the Spirulina, we added it three times a day to our drink. We went through our fast with flying colors. We will be doing this every six months now. We continue to use the three teaspoons of Spirulina each day. We would not want to be without it. We live on raw foods entirely. What a difference it makes in one's life.

Newberry Springs, CA

I just completed a Spirulina plankton fast (7 days) and I feel great. Thank you for your detailed explanation on how my body would react; it helped me understand the symptoms and enjoy the experience.

Greenacres, FL

Both my twin brother and myself were suffering from abdominal pains due to improper diet, exercise, etc. After fasting 10 days on Spirulina and liquids, with regular enemas, both of us feel that this is definitely worth inquiring about. It has given us a whole new outlook on living, period. The truth is always nice to know.

Libby, MT

I've been on a Spirulina and juice fast for the last three days and have been feeling incredible! I do believe the value of Spirulina is far beyond any food supplement I have ever come across and I have been looking for this type of thing for many years.

Beverly Hills, CA

Mother of two delighted

. . . [After reading a book *Rejuvenating the Body through Fasting with Spirulina Plankton*] . . . the very next morning I began my fast, that was six days ago.

Today I feel great! I'm delighted with the results I've achieved. My tongue is pink today and compared to my very first fast about 10 months ago I've had very little discomfort and have stayed active and vital. I'm married and have two young children, so vitality is necessary for me.

I still can hardly believe this is the sixth day of my fast. The first one, by the fourth day I thought I would die, but my nutritional counselor encouraged me to relax and finish purging my liver and gall bladder and keep to his diet directions and take an enema. Which I did, though I never thought I would bother fasting again. I'm so very glad I read [the] book; I wish I had done it sooner.

Scottsdale, AZ

This is the 2nd day of fast with Spirulina plankton powder which I am putting in gelatin capsules. Can't believe how good I feel, and am not hungry either.

Santa Fe, NM

I recently went on [a] fast with algae for seven days consuming only the algae and fruit juices. I was very much impressed with it and found it very satisfying. I noticed my attention span and concentration was increased only in a short time. I felt light and relaxed with no tension as a normal fast or diet leaves me. I also lost 8 pounds.

Stillwater, MN

I now look forward to fasting!! After fasting many years there was, before starting, always some apprehension because of some discomfort in the first few days.

After using Spirulina with the fast I can honestly say I experienced not one moment's discomfort. That is to me incredible, but after 14 days of fasting, my energy level was as high; no, it was higher than at the start; that is a minor miracle.

Philadelphia, PA

Chapter 7

JUST FEELING GREAT!

Spirulina is the answer to many a person who has complained, "I just don't feel good." In the letters that follow, a number of people report they feel a remarkable improvement in physical, emotional, and mental well-being after they have been taking Spirulina for only a short while. Spirulina is high in chlorophyll, which some call nature's "green blood" since it differs in composition by only one atom from the hemoglobin of human blood. As a result, eating Spirulina is an excellent way to nourish our very life blood with the nutrients that make it what it is. For some who eat Spirulina, it is the first time in their lives that they really receive the nutrition they need, and their letters acclaim they've never felt better.

"I no longer get tension headaches."

I have completed the 7 day fast with fruit juices and Spirulina plankton and have found the experience most rewarding. I HAVE NEVER FELT BETTER IN MY 33 YEARS OF LIFE! I lost 14 pounds I thought were a solid part of me -- I've never been fat -- I run 8 miles a day, 5 days a week and I no longer get tension headaches.

Schaumburg, IL

Spirulina is the perfect product. My sales seem to be doubling about every two weeks from repeats and the people they bring with them. I guess, we are all in the same predicament -- "Can't keep up with demand!"

Of course, I am using myself as example and I cannot tell you the blessings, physical and emotional, that Spirulina has brought me; and my customers see it too. Anyway, enough of this. I am a devout Christian who belongs to our Lord Jesus . . . I thank God for you and for Spirulina, and ask that He bless this great humanitarian venture that we have embarked upon. He *has already* and will continue to do so!!

Jacksonville, FL

I have used Spirulina all winter (4 mos. now) and I for one just love it -- aside from the 12 lbs. I lost -- I do not have to eat all that food, I never feel weak or hungry.

I am in *very* good health, I am 5'9" and weigh 140 lbs., had 6 kids, work each day of the year. I am 50 years old. I am sold on Spirulina plankton.

Dallas, TX

Personally, I have been taking Spirulina plankton for approximately one year and have been delighted with the results. While on a visit to Tyler earlier this year, I gave some Spirulina to some friends to try and they too were very pleased with it and have spread the good word among their friends.

Tyler, TX

I have been taking [X brand] Spirulina for about two months now and have noticed a big difference in the way I feel. I fasted for one week and lost about 7 pounds and have maintained that weight since. I have more energy and just feel good.

I wish to distribute Spirulina to my friends so they can feel as good as I do.

Belleville, IL

I am on [the] fasting with Spirulina diet. This is my fifth day. Today I am feeling great with plenty of energy. I am going to stay on it until my tongue is clear and all aches and pains are gone. I was 52 years old in June. I am very enthused about Spirulina.

Brandon, FL

"Psychological and physiological well-being."

I would like to express my enthusiasm and appreciation regarding the vitalizing and rejuvenating nature of [X brand]. Since using Spirulina, I have experienced a remarkably strong feeling of psychological and physiological well-being.

Denver, CO

I've been using Spirulina for the last five months and feel like a new person.

I find people interested in what has happened with me are now wanting Spirulina.

Tacoma, WA

I've just come off a 7 day fast and feel really great.

I am now taking the [. . .]* plankton, one teaspoon, morning and evening for rejuvenating the endocrine system.

Tucson, AZ

My husband and I have been taking Spirulina for about 4 months. We haven't even had a cold this winter. We are truck drivers and I have some of the other drivers on it now.

Graham, WA

I recently spent a month in Hawaii with a friend who is a Spirulina distributor. I had never heard of Spirulina plankton before, but she insisted I give it a try. I felt a gradual increase in energy until by the end of the bottle back home in Los Angeles I felt better than I can remember feeling, and I'm usually on the weak-sickly side.

Los Angeles, CA

"I feel so good."

Just the other day I felt the need for another fast. Overweight by over 5 to 10 lbs. affects me. A friend gave me the word on . . . Spirulina plankton. I am truly blessed! I feel so good. Many people are watching me, waiting for the fall, but never have I felt *so good*. I outwalked my 12 yr. old daughter recently and I am 38, but going on *20*.

In fact, at *20*, I did not enjoy benefits as good diet, proper supplements and now Spirulina.

Butler, PA

I take [Spirulina combined with amino acids] and absolutely have never felt better -- have had more energy, and better sleeping patterns.

Boulder Creek, CA

From the moment I was introduced to Spirulina I felt a familiar "ring". I guess people do, or don't, and if they *do*, it's to different degrees.

I don't express this to a whole lot of people, but I feel and have had a hunch that Spirulina is an evolutionary link—a transitionary factor. I believe it helps you maintain the highest frequency that a body has been able to open to. I've come to that conclusion based on experiences with my body and how it's changed or assisted it. I don't have the same body I started with 8 months ago!

It's incredible, the impact and changes I have seen in my customers' lives, too!

Red River, NM

"I feel fantastic."

I have been taking [X brand] Spirulina since August 1981. I read that for weight control I could take 7 tablets before each meal. I tend to be a compulsive eater and found the Spirulina extremely helpful! I feel fantastic.

Haverford, PA

Spirulina [with ginseng and bee pollen] has contributed greatly to my experience of physical aliveness. I want more of this product, I love it! It has changed my life.

Anaheim, CA

Thank you so much for [X brand] Spirulina. I know it's inspired. It has been like a miracle to all my family. Everyone feels better. Daily I talk to people who, with tears in their eyes, say thank you.

Portage, UT

Have been taking [. . .]* for more than a year and hope never to be without it, as I have so much more energy and my teeth have much improved from the wonderful minerals in [. . .]*. Own two books, *Rejuvenating the Body* and *The Secrets of Spirulina*. Have learned so much from them and am very grateful for the books and the wonderful Spirulina.

Santa Fe, NM

I have never been more impressed or enthusiastic about anything since my discovery of Spirulina. It has altered my health and consciousness over the past 8 months. It seemed to fine-tune my awareness of what is really important on this planet.

I have never in my life had any definite specific direction or goals that I eagerly pursued. I have always been very indecisive, which is cause for much confusion, bewilderment and depression. Recently I hit an all time low point in my life being unemployed and not having a grasp on reality in the city. Then my inner voice told me either end this existence or become the person you always somehow thought you could be and advance to your full potential. I began to fast with juice and Spirulina [with Vitamin C and cayenne] and also pray. After a couple of days a wonderful sense of well-being came over me. I had a vision of myself working side by side with beautiful people who were striving for God-consciousness working together in a harmonious environment. I have long dreamed of living heaven on Earth, even in these perilous times I always thought somewhere, somehow it was possible.

Portland, OR

"My figure is changing."

I'm 47 years old, just quit smoking and was afraid of gaining weight. Since I started using Spirulina I have been losing weight, my figure is changing and I have lots of energy. People in the hospital where I work are constantly commenting on the change they see in me. It's a wonderful feeling.

Los Altos, CA

Just a note to say how impressed I am with Spirulina. I started taking it a month ago and have so much more energy and have also lost weight. I have become a distributor and I get so excited to tell people about this wonderful Spirulina plankton.

Seattle, WA

I am now on my sixth day of fasting with 100% Pure Spirulina tablets and 3 to 4 glasses of fruit and vegetable juice per day. I feel so good; lots of energy and best of all, no craving for food. I am really sold on the benefits of [X brand].

Juneau, AK

I started using Plankton powder because of its vitamin content, plus the fact I cannot swallow a pill. The powder was a blessing in disguise; it mixes well with water and I can take it. After using Plankton powder for three months, I noticed an increase in my energy level. No more afternoon naps, and after dinner I still had energy to keep going with the kids. During this time I didn't snack between meals and I wasn't hungry. The end result was a 10 lb. weight loss. This was the easiest weight loss I ever had. I feel great!

Philadelphia, PA

Chapter 8

YOUNG PEOPLE, PETS & SUNDRY

Unlike us humans, with all the mental conditioning we have received from school, television, and friends about what foods are good and what are bad, animals have a keen innate sense of what is good for their bodies and what is not. Some of the delightful letters that follow describe the responses of animals to Spirulina—not merely their interest in the food—but their remarkable health improvements too. In fact many skeptics have "discovered" Spirulina after seeing what it has done for a beloved pet.

I started feeding my two cats Spirulina cat food approximately 2 weeks ago and have already noticed a dramatic improvement in the health and shine of their coats. They like their food much better when Spirulina is added to it, too. I feel that animals know what is naturally good for them to eat and they ate the Spirulina immediately.

Gainesville, FL

Abandoned kittens on Spirulina

I have had extreme success feeding my cats Spirulina. Cats in Northern California eat lizards in the summer and one of my cats almost died of starvation. I feed it [Spirulina with trace minerals] with some tuna and it is becoming fat again and in extremely good health. I am also feeding four baby kittens (that were abandoned by the mother) Spirulina and evaporated milk with a bottle and they are thriving.

Diamond Springs, CA

Both my cat and my gentleman friend have green eyes with black hair. Because of [. . .]*, both have lost the brown mineral deposits in their eyes (iridologically not surprising) and have full, rich black coats with much new shiny hair. He brought the Spirulina analysis to his professor, who immediately ordered a bottle of 200. This *is* a thinking person's food!

Also: I work in a law office. Our law clerk was up all night on speed for a final and stopped by the office for a few minutes before he rushed off in a daze. I said, "Here . . . take this!" I handed him 6 tabs of Spirulina and a few hours later he drove back from the University for the express purpose of telling me how absolutely tremendous he felt and that it was the only exam thus far that he'd aced! Like I said earlier, this *is* a thinking person's food.

Also: My mother is an oncologist (cancer nurse) and is totally excited about the possibilities of [. . .]* for the "starving" patient. Because of its immediate assimilability, the cancer can have no chance to rob the patient of the much needed nutrition.

I have many more stories, all equally exciting.

Venice, CA

Dog's skin condition disappears

I can offer you more pudding – I mean, proof. This is Yuki, our dog (Spitz) who is 12 years old. She used to get frequent indigestion. Her stomach would gurgle, and she would not eat. At such times, she would want to eat grass -- cats and dogs do that when they're sick. She also had for the past two years a bad skin condition under her paws. The skin was red, inflamed, and she licked them so much the hair disappeared and the inflamed skin was exposed. Some places in the recesses of the paws looked like red cockscomb. She licked her paws so much they would bleed. I spent several hundred dollars trying to cure this. A specimen was sent to the Veterinary School laboratory at UC-Davis, and the analysis said this was not an infection but an allergy of some kind.

In mid-February I started to feed her two tablets of Spirulina (total 1,000 mg). This is what happened:

1) No more indigestion problems. She doesn't try to eat grass anymore! (Spirulina is rich in chlorophyll.)
2) Her fur is radiant, soft and luxuriant. A noticeable improvement in condition of the hair. Absolutely!
3) Most amazingly, the awful skin condition in her paws has disappeared completely. She no longer licks or gnaws her paws, and the hair has grown back!

I took her to the vet for immunization shots, and she (the vet) couldn't believe her eyes. Especially the disappearance of that bad skin ailment. The vet checked the records and found that in 1980 a blood test indicated there was an unusually high level of a certain enzyme (produced by the liver, the name of which escapes me at the moment) that was eight times the normal level.

What has evidently happened is that [. . .]* has had a salubrious effect on the liver whose malfunction had been causing that skin condition. To me, there is no other explanation possible.

San Francisco, CA

I bought a jar of [dog food with Spirulina] for my cocker spaniel. She has been troubled terribly by fleas, and I am convinced that parasites are a symptom of a generally weakened physical condition. I have noticed a general improvement in her energy level and have only spotted one flea since I've been giving her 2 teaspoons of [X brand] each day. And the sores above her tail are definitely better.

Orange, CA

Youth returns to chocolate poodle

Bob has a close friend by the name of "Charlie Brown". Poor Charlie has arthritis of the spine and is under a doctor's supervision and care.

For many months, Charlie could do little more than pull and wobble around. In September 1981 Bob gave Charlie some Spirulina powder, which Charlie greatly loved and would go around with a nice green tongue after eating the Spirulina powder. When Bob ran out of the powder, Charlie was just as satisfied with the tablets.

To make a long story longer, Charlie is a chocolate poodle that is 17 years old and is now acting like a 2 year old. Charlie even went out to romp with the youngsters (something he has not done in years). Bob says Charlie owes his new found energy and youth to [. . .]* [and] says "Thanks" to everyone. Bob says he has authority to speak in behalf of Charlie.

Naples, FL

I have been feeding my long haired dachshund from ¼ to ½ teaspoon of [cat food with Spirulina] along with his other food. He acquired a cataract over the one eye, completely covering it. There seemed nothing nutritionally that could be done. A $500.00 cataract removal operation is too high for me. After 4 months, some brown is beginning to show through the cataract. I seriously doubt if the Spirulina will remove the cataract, but it is helping the dog. He had back problems from a fall down a canyon. The dog now sits up and runs around. His hair was only partially grown out and now he has long hair all over his body. He is a long haired dachshund from Germany. I believe the Spirulina has helped him.

Seattle, WA

A friend's dog was bitten by a cotton mouth. It swelled up and was dying. After giving it 12 [. . .]* the swelling started going down and by the next day the dog was in good shape, but for good measure we gave it some more.

Spirulina is so great, I wish I could turn more people on to it.

Willow Springs, MO

We had a seven year old German shepherd that my son said was just like a brother to him. This last September he died from a tick disease. We had bred him to a female shepherd not knowing he was sick. We now have two of his pups and I vowed to keep them as healthy as I possibly could. When I ordered the Spirulina from my health food store I also ordered the Spirulina for dogs. They have it daily with their regular diet and I am so glad to relate that they both have very shiny coats and are so full of energy. And they shall continue to have it included in their daily diet. I am grateful to know of these benefits.

Canton, TX

Yes, I am most pleased with the results of [. . .]*. My German shepherd has really improved for the better, not only his coat but his total health condition. We had a slight skin condition prior to using [Spirulina]. I can truthfully say, it has cleared up and he rests in comfort now, but I can see the big difference in his eyes -- they are really clear now and beautifully alert.

El Segundo, CA

"Our dog loves Spirulina."

I have just become acquainted with Spirulina. It was like the answer to a prayer. I have always been an advocate of proper nutrition and fasting, but the last two years I have put on 20 unwanted pounds.

Our dog loves Spirulina. Plan to feed the kids on it when they get home from camp. I would like to sell it direct to my friends and maybe even trade distribution.

Boston, MA

Already I'm feeling more energy and well-being. I love the Spirulina plankton powder in the juices I drink, sprout juice and apple juice and also on my food. My little dog likes it too, sprinkled on his food.

Kingman, AZ

My horse is really doing well on that [X brand] pelleted Spirulina. Not only does she look nice but her attitude reflects it. Most tack available today is designed to force the horse to perform by inflicting pain as a punishment for disobedience. I ride without a bit, spurs, or a crop/whip. A horse that feels good is willing to perform and my horse seems to reflect that. One of these days I'll send a picture of a Spirulina-fed horse.

Sturgeon Bay, WI

I have been on [X brand] Spirulina for three months now and feel so much younger it is unbelievable. I have so much energy and my thinking and dreams are improving so rapidly, I will never do anything but to promote Spirulina for everyone.

I have started feeding Spirulina to my pets. I have three bull snakes and one diamondback rattlesnake and one small lizard. I have them all on Spirulina; like myself, they do not live entirely on it, but I put the Spirulina in their water and leave enough in their cage so they are covered with Spirulina most of the time on their skins.

Alamogordo, NM

Extra energy for the athlete!

I am an all-American and a nationally top ranked athlete in one of the most demanding sports, wrestling. I am also a senior at Oregon State University. I went through a 12 day fast. The reason for my fast was to clean my body of the toxins and to help my meditation in becoming a national champion. I have had great success, I became more energetic, my concentration and meditation improved also. I am to the point where I know my body functions very well under stress with Spirulina plankton. I want to continue the use of this most complete food because it works in harmony with the demanding sport of wrestling and my meditation.

Corvallis, OR

I am now taking [Spirulina with ginseng, bee pollen, and niacin] with very positive results.

I have been involved in professional baseball the last six years. My baseball pursuits put me in contact with a great number of people that would be very interested in [X brand].

Phoenix, AZ

I took Spirulina for 3 months while training in a running team. My racing improved over the three month time very much. I raced at the end of my three month time and went on a three day Spirulina fast and ran my fastest race ever. I know it was the Spirulina because I have been racing for 12 years and it is the only diet change that has helped this much.

Boulder Creek, CA

Since taking Spirulina, I have stopped smoking, am training for a Triathlon, have won running medals, and have noticed my life and outlook soaring. So many people have asked me about Spirulina, I was encouraged to write up [an] article.

Emeryville, CA

I'm a faithful user of Spirulina as a daily supplement and have also fasted on it several times. As a runner, bicyclist, and cross-country skier, I have felt its healthful effects and have acquainted friends in my community with its potential.

Jackson, WY

After divorce and depression—

At long last came along . . . Spirulina. It has changed my life completely for the better! I can think clearly once more and remember better. And best of all I am getting back to my old, creative self as a poet and journalist and public relations specialist.

Even more important, I seem to be stronger now and more energetic in speaking out for my rights! I've been too long acquiescent, sadly lacking in personal punch. Therefore no one -- not even my former husband has shown me regard, much less respect, in any matter.

My daughter in San Jose, Calif., has benefitted greatly from Spirulina.

Wichita, KS

Myself: retired restaurant owner, active bowler and golfer, excellent health especially so since starting to use [X brand] products 5 months ago. Initially started with [Spirulina combined with bee pollen, ginseng, and combined with niacin as well as] 100% Spirulina. Experimented and found that, for me, various combinations of [Spirulina with niacin, Vitamin C, cayenne, ginseng and bee pollen] work the best.

Wife: active real estate salesperson, uses [. . .]* and some 100%. She is very pleased with the extra energy and weight control she achieves.

Son: experimented with [. . .]* to help teen-age acne. Tried [. . .]* (one daily) and [. . .]* and achieved better results.

Son: his combination is one [Spirulina with niacin], 2 to 6 [Spirulina with ginseng] and some bee pollen. His hobby is marathon running and he trains an average of ten to fifteen miles daily. In the last few months he has completed the Honolulu, Maui and Seoul marathons in successively better times and has decreased his times in his training runs. He is an outstanding example of the benefits to be derived from using [Spirulina] products.

Daughter: nursing student, uses [Spirulina with niacin, ginseng, bee pollen, comfrey], 100% Spirulina, and [Spirulina with multiple vitamins]. Satisfactory results.

Fredonia, NY

"I was never happy before taking Spirulina."

I am 15 years old and am practically living on plankton. I watch very much what I eat. I started watching what I ate not too long ago because I couldn't digest a lot of foods.

I was never happy before I started taking Spirulina. I was always depressed and I tried to even kill myself several times, but it seemed to never work.

Heppner, OR

I have just started college.

I want to say I really like Spirulina. I have never been into health foods, but I decided to try [. . .]* as an energy booster. It really works. I have also noticed that I require 2–3 hours less sleep.

Before I started taking Spirulina I hated lettuce and salads. Now I love salads. I also had high blood pressure 158/90; now it is down to 130/57, a big drop in about a month.

Pinkhill, NC

Gives up marijuana after taking Spirulina

Speaking purely of my own experiences, I can say [X brand] Spirulina has had the greatest effect in my life of any single physical factor. But by no means has that effect been restricted to my physical life. For the first time in 12 years I am *not* compelled to use marijuana -- in fact I feel its time is long past. I have been feeling "controlled" by pot for a very long time now. But after taking fairly large amounts of Spirulina (12–25 tabs a day and some powder) I rejoice in my determination and ability to desist.

A large part (if not all) of this new ability is attributable to a Great Factor. I have come much closer to the One Almighty God. I am 100% positive [X brand] Spirulina is the force behind this. My mind and heart have been opened and positive and faithful energies have poured in.

My wife and I are closer with more love and understanding for each other. I love her so much; it pleases me to know we can work it out with good judgement and God's gift of health and wisdom: Spirulina.

I will add one more blessing received of Spirulina. This is *more* important than my own feelings. My beautiful daughter (and future kids) will grow up whole and healthy with Spirulina. She is 18 months old now. She *loves* Spirulina; eating 5 to 10 grams a day.

Knoxville, TN

Well, I've just attained nirvana, or samadhi, or mystical heights of bliss, all due to Spirulina plankton!! I'd better quit rambling before you think I'm some sort of "kelp spy" or something! (Could you imagine me writing a letter like this to IBM or SEARS???? Well, maybe someday!)

Fort Wayne, IN

I have the minister and his family off to a good start using Spirulina. I'm also talking to the congregation about my personal experiences with "Manna from Heaven."

National City, CA

It was revealed to me by divine revelation that Spirulina plankton is the super survival food for men in the 1980's. I now have thicker scalp or head of hair, better elimination, calmer nerves, and plenty of physical energy. I also had piles and they are healed and just about gone.

Chicago, IL

Chapter 9

ADVANCING YEARS

LE ONARDO
VINCI

> *Many older people are thrilled to report a return to youthful vigor on Spirulina. Health improvement, weight loss, energy uplift, and even increased alertness and sharpness of the senses are among their testimonies.*

This past winter, my mother was told by her doc - poor health. Behind her back he told me she did not have long to live. Daughter Nancy put her on Spirulina, along with colon treatment, which she taught me how to do for her, plus watching diet. This summer her doctor, wanting to know what she has been doing, found her health improved 99 or, I should say, 100%. She is 76 years old, diabetic 20 years - had one kidney removed 23 years ago. Today she is driving herself to all places - senior citizen clubs; also selling Spirulina to friends. Before Spirulina, she did not have strength to walk around one block! My 27-year old son also experienced great *(sic)* with it; rode a bike 70 miles, along the way legs were paining to the point - got off bike - took out his tablets - Spirulina, [in] 12–15 minutes was able to finish his 70 mile trip with no pain.

My experience - looking better, more energy, other customers tell me the same. A few negatives - a few afraid to try something new.

Ardsley, NY

I am the complete advocate of Spirulina! I have made it my total food for periods of up to 60 days, and other times with minimal fruit and vegetable additions.

Spirulina became available at a time when I was redoing my life. Now at 66, I feel my best years are ahead, thanks in part to finding a satisfactory food source.

Big Harbor, WA

The luckiest moment

There have been several, shall I say, lucky moments in my seventy-one years, but I believe, up until now, the luckiest one ever was when I read the article on Spirulina in the June issue of the National Enquirer. I said, that's for me. I got in my car, drove 15 miles . . . and bought some.

I have lost 8 lbs. but still have a long way to go . . . I feel better, I breathe better, I walk better; hell, if I felt any better, I couldn't stand it!

Van Buren, AR

My brain was "on fire"

After losing a dear wife after 70 years of happiness, I am 92, became very ill. Was told it was depression. It is true, a certain part of me was down in spirits, but my thinking was not correct and writing became difficult, with no pain anywhere in my entire body. Thought my end was close and just about gave up. My daughter put me on Spirulina, 2nd day at mealtime. Noticed nothing much for about ten days, but suddenly found myself back in a thinking mood that was entirely different. Called my daughter on the phone and told her my brain was "on fire." A 100% change in my thinking and a joy to feel so much better, which today I can hardly understand. Everyone says, "What a miracle." But am afraid, will have to give the credit to Spirulina.

Tustin, CA

From early teen-age it has been evident that my body metabolism has been malfunctioning. My parents attempted through various specialists to have the condition corrected. All were unsuccessful. Inasmuch as I am now sixty-nine years old, and my own continuously seeking relief through proper nutrition and medical means was without any particular results, I have been overjoyed to attain marked improvement in only fifteen days of using the Spirulina.

Oxnard, CA

I have now been on Spirulina for 4 months and have been able to lose weight that I could not take off before. I went off Spirulina for a week to see what would happen. I not only gained the weight I lost, but put on a few more, so I went back on it and took off everything I had gained. But this is not as important to me as the natural energy that I get from [. . .]*. I used to be a high energy person but, as age comes, energy seems to go. Not so with [. . .]*; it has given me energy I had so long ago in my youth. This is the main reason I take it, as it gives me a natural feeling of just being good, and the energy to take care of my duties as a housewife.

San Jose, CA

I have been sick with stomach problems for years. I am 59 years old. I have been on nutrition for [the] past 10 years.

I was allergic to soybean and different diets I have been on. I could never lose weight and feel good.

Since I have found [X brand] Spirulina, I have lost 8 lbs., 4 inches. I can eat salad now. I feel better than I have felt in years. I am not craving sweets like I was. I sure wouldn't ever want to be without. Also I have more energy.

Norwalk, CA

Sight and hearing improved!

I purchased my first order of Spirulina August 16, 1981. On September 1, I became a distributor. By September 15, I had lost 13 pounds, felt great, had energy to burn and was never hungry.

I noticed my eyes quit stinging and watering, so when I took my driving test to renew my license, I left my glasses off and passed reading the top line - so after 30 years of wearing glasses to drive, I no longer have to.

The following morning I discovered I could hear my 15 year old wrist watch tick - for the *1st* time.

My retired (2 years) husband wants to go back to work as he is no longer tired. I did go back to work "telling" Spirulina.

I could go on and on - but enough for now.

Mt. Vernon, WA

I have lost 20 lbs. and I had trouble with my legs all the time, they swelled and were hurting. Since I have been taking plankton, no more problems.

The veins are almost normal. I feel great. Thank God for the Spirulina . . . I am 64 years old and I never found anything that would come close to plankton. I was at the Dr.'s every week, and now once a month is great.

Best relief anyone could have. I have more pep than I ever dreamed of at my age.

Portland, OR

Our family, mother, 73, husband, 61, and me, 54, have been on Spirulina for about three weeks. . . . It's wonderful!

We've all done fine, but with the use of Spirulina, it's really going "great guns", losing weight too.

Jasper, TX

I have been able to closely observe dramatic improvements in others that I have recommended Spirulina to. The results in all cases have been very positive. In my dealings with people I come in contact with many older people, a great deal older than myself, who are in various states of physical and emotional decay. [. . .]* has most definitely improved their mental and physical outlook. They, in turn, have told their friends about it and word of mouth is strong advertising indeed.

Richmond, B.C., Canada

Dramatic improvements

I have fasted on [X brand] algae and there is nothing like it.

I have a Rest Home with 15 elderly people. Since I have experienced the unbelievable benefits of Spirulina on myself, I would like to feed it to everybody, also my help and the many people I come in contact with — even to my friends and relatives in Europe.

Olivenhain, CA

Chapter 10

PROBLEMS

It's only fair to present the other side of the story. Some people do not fare well on Spirulina. The percentage of letters received in this category was very small. Some of them are included here along with suggestions from the editor as to why their bodies had a negative response to Spirulina rather than a positive one. In some cases suggestions are made as to how to rightly use Spirulina. There are, of course, many brands of Spirulina on the marketplace. It is important to select one which laboratory tests have shown is no phoney—100% pure Spirulina with no additives or fillers.

I am very unhappy with the results that I have gotten . . . (with Spirulina). I have tried to follow your dosage and plan but to no avail.

Indio, CA

Editor's Note: Some people fail with their new nutritional program simply because they don't understand how their body works. They think they were in better condition with their old habits and diet before they took Spirulina. But this is because they have not given the body a chance to adjust and to cleanse and restore worn-out tissues with the supernutrition that Spirulina is providing. If they had only persisted a little while longer, they would have begun to feel better than before they started. The power of the body is actually increased, but this increased energy is being sent first to the vital internal organs that need to be vitalized and reconstructed. Weakness which is felt during this initial period is not real weakness but merely a regathering of forces for the rebuilding of important internal parts. Many people never go through this phase, but if we do, it is essential for us to stop wasting energy, to rest and sleep more, and to realize that the years of improper diet are the only reason for our discomfort and that the body is receiving a blessing during this crucial phase. After a short time of patience we will get increased strength which will exceed by far what we felt before we began the new program.

The enclosed unused portion of Plankton Powder makes me ill when I take it. Is there something wrong with it? If so, please let me know. . . . . My experience with it precludes my trying it again, I fear.

Richland, WA

Editor's Note: Many people do not realize that they may experience symptoms and changes when they introduce foods and supplements of a higher quality, such as Spirulina, in place of lower quality ones that have been a part of their diet. The less refined the food you eat, the closer it is to the way it is found in nature, the higher its quality. All enzymes are intact and all the protein-forming amino acids are present in their finest form when foods are left in this raw, unfired condition, not to mention the minerals, vitamins, trace elements, carbohydrates and "life force". Assimilating and properly digesting higher-quality foods enables the body to discard lower grade materials and tissues to make room for the superior materials which it uses to make new and healthier tissues. When we first begin this process by introducing substances such as Spirulina, which are more alive and more natural than we are accustomed to, we may experience headaches and/or a letdown. This can occur not only because our body is directing more energy than usual into a rebuilding process, but also because the body is discarding toxins which are removed from the tissues and transported through the bloodstream during its many bodily rounds. Before these noxious agents reach their final destination for elimination, they may cause us some discomfort which will usually last no more than three days. We will then feel stronger as our health and energy rise up to an entirely new level.

When I started using Spirulina I noticed constipation, though before long this symptom went away. One of my distributors complained of diarrhea at first, though now she is very regular. I'm confused.

Boulder Creek, CA

I purchased a bottle of Spirulina Plankton and the pills do not work for me. They not only made me nauseated, but they made me so full of gas and caused constipation. I stopped taking them for a while and tried them again, but had the same problems. I feel it must be the iron in them. I cannot take iron very well. Do these pills come without iron? Is my complaint normal? I feel I wasted my money and I am sorry I can't use them . . . I was taking 6 pills a day at first, then cut back to 3 pills, but still had the problem.

Sunnyvale, CA

Editor's Note: Some bodies are very sensitive to any changes in diet. If a person has never taken Spirulina before, and they suddenly introduce this high-powered source of nutrition to their system, either diarrhea or constipation can result. Such people need to begin gradually with Spirulina and allow their bodies time to adjust. Oftentimes the simple solution to the constipation problem is to increase the intake of liquid, so necessary for the proper assimilation of the increase in protein in the diet or to increase the intake of fiber. It is important to remember that everyone's digestive processes and nutritional history are different, and they may get the opposite results when trying the same food for the first time.

I've fasted for 7 days on . . (Spirulina) . . and saw remarkable results in my physical and spiritual well-being. However, I seem to have a problem with gas and that did not, as of yet, dissipate. There seem to be so many possible causes of this disorder that I don't know where to begin when I think of eliminating it.

Edneyville, NC

Editor's Note: A gas problem could well be a reaction of Spirulina with poor intestinal flora. After fasting with Spirulina for a time the intestinal flora may undergo a change. If enemas are not taken during the fast, one may accumulate a lot of toxic matter in the colon that can cause gas. In this case enemas with distilled water are needed or a colonic. New "friendly" digestive bacteria can then be re-introduced by ingesting an acidophilus or Bifidus culture. If one has taken enemas with chlorinated tap water as part of his/her fasting program, the chlorine in the water could have destroyed the natural bacteria balance, thus triggering the gas problem. Again, the re-introduction of helpful bacteria would be most beneficial. Emotional pressure can be another cause of gas. A crinkling up of the stomach can occur, resulting in greater fermentation and pressuring of gas into the colon. In this case, drinking more liquids will bring relief.

Another possible reason is drinking fruit juices with a very high natural sugar content. Fresh-squeezed juices are always best if available; if not, relying more on citrus and vegetable juices could eliminate the problem.

I have a customer who has tried Spirulina a few different times recently, but has had to discontinue use because of sores that erupt in her nose! Poor lady! She really likes Spirulina otherwise, she feels it curbs her appetite, but these sores are painful and ugly!

Tigard, OR

Editor's Note: Spirulina does encourage the elimination of toxins. We do not know what this lady's diet was, but she may have accumulated toxins in her body which later came out as sores. A diet of raw food for a week or so could help prepare this woman for Spirulina, which she could try again after that time with one tablet before each meal.

I am very unhappy with the effects of . . . (Spirulina Plankton Powder) which have included nausea, dizziness and stomach cramps.

Richmond, VA

Editor's Note: Spirulina powder does not agree with some people due to the smell and color, in which case the tablets might agree with them better. It is also possible that this person may be one of the rare people who are allergic to something in this natural product, just as there are some people who are allergic to milk, eggs, chocolate, etc.

Chapter 11

RIGHT TO THE POINT

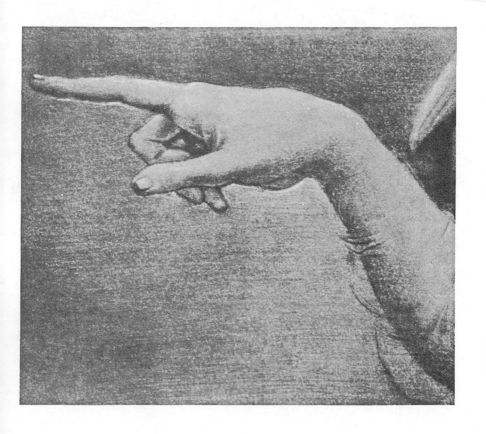

Sometimes just a few words are all it takes to convey how good it feels to be taking Spirulina!

I totally believe in the product.

Hollywood, CA

I'm already taking Spirulina and find it fascinating! Fabulous energy and well-being.

Marina del Ray, CA

Spirulina is indeed a powerful food and I am taking one (1) heaping tablespoon daily.

Santa Barbara, CA

I am convinced of Spirulina. It's great!

Elkino, WV

I am using Spirulina now and find it extraordinary.

Chicago, IL

. . . have met up with an overwhelming enthusiasm for Spirulina. Truly, it is an amazing food!

Kelly, WY

I personally use Spirulina and received many benefits.

Xenia, OH

I began using it [Spirulina] myself with impressive results . . .

Chicago, IL

I have just started taking Spirulina and am amazed of the results already.

Palmer, AK

[. . .]* has completely cured the pain in my left side that has cost me a few hundred dollars to find out from the doctors. Truly amazing!

Moro, OR

Wonderful stuff . . . am having excellent results.

Phippsburg, CO

I am at present using it [Spirulina] for myself and I am so excited about the results, I want to tell all my friends about it.

San Jose, CA

I feel uplifted throughout the day. I have a good deal of energy even at the end of the day.

Boulder Creek, CA

I have tried [X brand] Spirulina and am quite happy with the results so far. I am going into my fourth day of fasting which for me is a record.

Anchorage, AK

I started [taking Spirulina] June 17th and have lost 13 lbs. and feel great. I'm sold on Spirulina!

Shafter, CA

I believe we have one of the greatest products [Spirulina] God has seen fit to offer mankind.

Auburn, AL

I and many of my friends fast regularly with the plankton and we all feel it has done wonders.

Bloomington, IL

I am very much impressed by the effectiveness of [X brand].

Annapolis, CA

I've recently started using Spirulina and find it's a great food.

Eugene, OR

I've had fantastic results with Spirulina in my work.

Strasburg, OH

I have been taking Spirulina for the past six months with good results; I have never felt better or had more energy.

Hattiesburg, MS

I've just the past two weeks been introduced to Spirulina plankton and I'm very impressed.

Rupert, ID

I am especially interested in finding [Spirulina with niacin]. I found it gave me energy and I felt great.

Palm Springs, CA

After having recently finished my 7-day fast (7 days and 13½ hours) I am very enthused about Spirulina.

Pompano Beach, FL

I have been using Spirulina for just a month and I have already experienced excellent results.

N. Hollywood, CA

I have been using the 100% plankton powder for some time now and am sold on it myself.

Fresno, CA

My wife and I have been using Spirulina for five months now. Our health is vibrant, both in body and spirit.

Walnut Creek, CA

I am using it [Spirulina plankton] and it is excellent.

Mobile, AL

I have been taking Spirulina now for about 2 weeks and already notice that I sleep better, have greatly decreased dandruff, and a sharper mind.

Burley, ID

I have a severe chronic nutritional deficiency, so the tablets are insufficient for my needs, but the powder is a big help.

Detroit, MI

I was just introduced to it [Spirulina] a few short weeks ago and am so impressed with it. I since have started one of my daughters and her 2 sons (ages 4 and 8) on it.

Grand Junction, CO

I am very pleased and astonished at the results of my taking Spirulina and would like to receive any material pertaining to this vitamin.

Tampa, FL

My friend gave me some [X brand]* and it suppressed my desire to drink.

Hood River, OR

I have used Spirulina for about three weeks and feel much better and have more energy.

Las Vegas, NV

I have been using [X brand] Spirulina since last year and have been delighted with it.
It's lovely stuff.

Southall MIDDX, England

This [. . .]* also helps my arthritis.

San Jose, CA

I used [X brand] Spirulina and am very pleased with the results. Therefore I want to continue using and selling it.

Phoenix, AZ

This "Manna" is *Miraculous*! After my 21 day fast I'll write more!

Bellaire, TX

I have diabetes and I feel that [. . .]* are helping my problem.

Boise, ID

I am a diabetic and these pills are the only thing that keeps my sugar down in tape test.

Heppner, OR

I have just been introduced to Spirulina plant plankton. After only 4 days of 6 tablets per day I surely feel better.

Hibbing, MN

[After five days of fasting . . .]

I have never felt better and have had *NO* hunger *ever*! It's great.

Newport Beach, CA

Spirulina is fantastic!

Houston, TX

My husband and I are taking Spirulina on a fast at present. We are thrilled with the way it is acting on us . . .

Galt, CA

I feel I have just discovered a true path of health.

Geyserville, CA

I like it very much and feel it does something for me.

Mukwonago, WI

For several months I've been using these wonderful products. I am very pleased with the results.

New York, NY

Have lost the pangs of hunger and lost weight and been satisfied.

Santa Maria, CA

I am presently taking [Spirulina with Vitamin C and cayenne]. I feel absolutely great!

Indianapolis, IN

I am impressed with the energy I personally have received from [X brand] Plankton powder.

Calistoga, CA

. . . my sister has used it for one week now and lost 5 lbs. and feels great.

Oxnard, CA

Spirulina is great! I like the results I get from using it.

Albuquerque, NM

Sure am enjoying that Spirulina!

Summerfield, NC

I have been very happy with my personal discovery of Spirulina. It is a dietary GOD SEND.

Los Gatos, CA

I have been using Spirulina for the past month and am impressed by its effectiveness and potential.

San Pedro, CA

I have personally been selling and using Spirulina for about 6 months now and find it to be an *excellent* food supplement.

Las Vegas, NV

I just finished a 7 day fast using it [Spirulina] and juices and feel wonderful.

San Francisco, CA

I am feeling so much better since I have been taking them [Spirulina] and want to know more about Spirulina and plankton.

Piedra, CA

You're right - there is absolutely nothing like Spirulina. My wolf-hound and I now run 6 miles a day.

Mound, MN

Chapter 12

WHAT DOCTORS & OTHER HEALTH PROFESSIONALS ARE SAYING

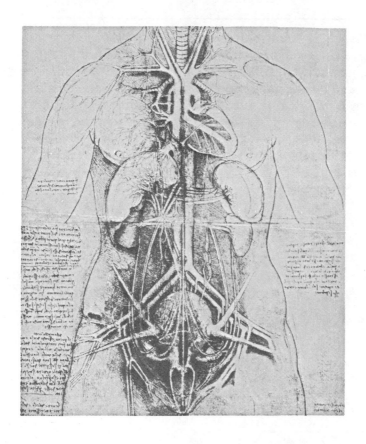

Although the FDA considers Spirulina a food and therefore prevents individuals from making medical claims for its benefits, people are finding out for themselves what Spirulina can do. Many doctors and other health professionals have been quick to discover the benefits of Spirulina, both using it personally and in their practices. We have asked several of them to contribute a statement on their experiences with Spirulina, to add the unique perspective of the medical professional to the wide array of human experience we have presented here.

Spirulina is one of the quickest and most easily assimilated forms of protein. I use it myself.

Dr. Robert Picker
Berkeley, CA

During 1982 I have had twenty clients who have had a low cobalt on the trace mineral analysis by hair, all at two standard deviations below the mean. Cobalt is obtained in the body via Vitamin B-12. These people were vegetarians and started taking Spirulina, either putting the powder on their food or by taking capsules with their meals. They were re-checked ninety days after consuming daily intake of Spirulina and in all instances the cobalt had returned to within a normal reference range.

Sincerely,
C. Jean Poulos, Sc.D., Ph.D.
Registered Nutrition Specialist
Santa Cruz, CA

I am taking this opportunity to inform you about my private success, concerning the use of "Spirulina" grown in Israel for dieting. For years I tried to lose weight, by all kinds of methods, even "Weight Watchers," and it did not help me, until I started with the Spirulina. During three months I lost almost 10 pounds without any problem and no headache. I personally am very, very pleased with the [. . .]*; especially it helps me to work on a long day without feelings of either hunger or headache, which is for me important.

Respectfully,
Dr. Sh. Weissman, Director
Institute for Food Microbiology, Ltd.
Haifa, ISRAEL

When I saw my listless, tired, and fat friend becoming less listless, and less tired, and "Oh God, No!" less fat than I was, I kind of panicked. I took her by the shoulders, and I shook her, and I said, "What are you doing to make you look so good?!" She told all. And I met Spirulina.

I saw summer in at a whopping 175 lbs. Petite for basketball, but too large for a tu-tu. At Christmas, I was down to 135, and even though I was too late to learn my part for the Nutcracker Suite, I had my best Christmas yet. A new me.

If I were the world's messenger, I'd want the world to know that Spirulina was my answer to losing weight and keeping it lost, and feeling good, and being happy. And I know if God sends answers to prayers and tears, then God sent someone to me who gave me Spirulina. And maybe I can repay that prayer by giving it back to the rest of the world.

No human is gently touched by someone or something that somewhere it's not repaid. I would never withhold my joy of being "finally thin enough" without the desire to see every man or woman as thin, and as happy with themselves as I am. It's a gift received, returned. Maybe I can do that. Maybe I can help.

I'm a nurse. And every day I see that pain in the eyes of my patients who grow sick because obesity and malnutrition thrive, and health and vitality have found a very dark place to hide. And I have succumbed to their pain, because it has also been my pain, and I could not help them because I could not help myself. Now I take care of them in an even better way than I was able to before. When they see my energy, and my enthusiasm, and my love for "living" life, they want to know. And I have a wonderful story to tell them.

Dusty Minton, R.N.
Carrollton, TX

My name is Susan Gosink. I am a Licensed Vocational Nurse with fifteen years of hospital nursing experience. My husband, Alan Gosink, is a Licensed Psychiatric Technician with ten years of in-hospital experience in mental health counseling and has a B.A. in psychology. He is currently on leave-of-absense from R.N. school. We both have been studying natural methods of healing and prevention, on our own, for a number of years.

Last December (1981) we embarked on a journey of good health that has proven to be the most incredible experience of our lives. In November we began supplementing our diet with Spirulina plankton. The last two weeks of November, we began a cleansing diet primarily of fruits, vegetables and Spirulina plankton. Starting the first of December, we began our Spirulina fast, consisting of Spirulina tablets, a small amount of lecithin granules and fresh fruit and vegetable juices. During the first month we assisted the cleansing process with daily doses of herbal intestinal cleansers and daily enemas. We are still on our wonderful Spirulina journey which numbers just past 9½ months to date. We are feeling so wonderful we plan to continue at least until December 1, 1982 which will make the fast one year.

The benefits we have received from this experience are varied and numerous. I have included just the highlights here.

Physically, we have changed considerably. I have lost forty pounds and changed from a size 14 dress to an 8. Alan lost fifty pounds and went from an extra-large shirt size to a medium. Our skin has become soft and clear and we have a visible glow of health that is apparent to all who observe us. We lost all of the weight in the first four months and stabilized within a week of each other. Our weight now varies up or down only two or three pounds in a month. We are experiencing a new energy level that surpasses anything we have ever known. We have a very full schedule and for the first time in our lives we have more than enough energy to meet the demands of our busy lives. I am a full-time nurse at Methodist Hospital here in Sacramento. Alan works full-time sharing Spirulina with hundreds of new friends. We have two sons, ages 5 and 9, who are healthy and active. They both eat a Spirulina-supplemented vegetarian diet.

Mentally we have experienced some real changes. We have experienced an increase in clarity of mind and an improvement in memory.

I have experienced a real improvement in my reaction time. (When I drop something, I am usually able to catch it again mid-air. This is a new experience for me.)

Alan has had hypoglycemia for most of his life. Since being on this fast, the biggest improvement for him, mentally, has been the absence of mood-swings, anger, hyper-sensitivity, and other troublesome symptoms of the hypoglycemic syndrome. Never before has he been able to speak in public because of his stress reactions, which were so bad at times that he would lose his voice and have severe heart palpitations. Since fasting we have had numerous T.V. and radio appearances. He has done several as well, by himself. All this stress—without a stress reaction!

Spiritually, we both have grown beyond measure. Fasting for increased spiritual awareness is an age-old practice. We cannot begin to express the depth of the blessings we have received throughout this fast.

We have been monitored by two medical doctors throughout this fast. We have had several physical examinations and several sets of lab work. Both physicians have found us to be in remarkably good health. In fact, they have been so impressed with what they have observed that they both use [. . .]* in their diet daily and have stated that they would not be without it due to the energy boost it gives them in their busy lives. At Methodist Hospital, eight doctors and twenty-five or thirty nurses have used [. . .]* and were very impressed with this energy-giving food!

Alan and I are now actively trying to promote Spirulina as the answer to the world hunger problem. Any food, which when taken in the small amounts we have taken, can give us the incredible quality of life we are now experiencing, has to be an answer to world hunger. We are both very committed to sharing this reality with as many as possible to help bring about world-wide production to feed our hungry planet. We are concerned about the hungry overseas as well as the nutritionally starved here in America who are losing their birth-right of good health on a diet of highly processed foods. Eating Spirulina, which is at the bottom of the food chain, is ecologically sound for all of us on this planet, which faces severe food shortages in the not-too-distant future. We are so excited and feel so blessed to offer this fast for all to see as living testimony of the incredible nutritional value of Spirulina Plankton.

Susan Gosink, L.V.N.
Sacramento, CA

Following is her doctor's observation . . . May 20, 1982

I have observed Alan and Susan Gosink during the period of time beginning December 1, 1981 and continuing through the present date. During this time they state they have been on a self-imposed nutritional program consisting of fruit and vegetable juices, herb teas, bran fiber, [X brand] Spirulina Plankton and [X brand] lecithin granules exclusively.

I have monitored them by occasional observation, periodical laboratory blood analysis and by physical examination and do find them to be in good health.

This statement is not a professional endorsement of their nutritional program but rather a statement that in my professional opinion they have been and do continue to be in good health while on this nutritional program.

Barbara J. Nash, M.D.
Sacramento, CA

In reply to your request for my opinion of Spirulina Plankton, and with the understanding that this is my personal endorsement only: I have been involved in the field of wholistic healing for some thirty years and exposed to the many facets of the healing arts.

Having an awareness of the individuality of bio-chemical and bio-electrical make-up of each person, I offer my personal experience. I have been using a limited amount of Spirulina tablets (about 6 per day) for 90 days. In this period I have been able to cut down on the amount of my usual supplement requirements and am experiencing a "high" in energy flow and a sense of well-being, in spite of it being a period of unusual stress.

As a bonus, I find that I have lost 2 inches off my waistline without losing any weight. I am blessed with being in the normal weight range even though I am at the age of 58.

At this point, I do not miss the daily opportunity to recommend Spirulina products to both patients and friends.

Sincerely yours,
s/s Robert E. Shaffer, Ph.D.
Managing Editor
International Academy
of Nutritional Consultants
Huntington Beach, CA

Spirulina is an ideal way to avoid the junk food habit. Rather than crashing down on a plate of potato chips in the afternoon, the busy person can take Spirulina when hungry or wanting more energy.

Most people violate their bodies and do not regard the common good health practices of enough exercise, rest, right diet, and relaxation. Then they go to their doctors and expect instant health. But health is a way of life. And Spirulina is a way to maintain the correct weight with a diet that is balanced, an essential factor in the health of the human system.

Vegetarians find it very hard to get a balanced diet. They almost have to have their own cooks, if they are busy people, if they are to get all the proteins they need. Spirulina is a real breakthrough for them because its protein content and variety of amino acids provides the quick, natural nutrition they need without eating meat.

I myself have been using Spirulina for about a year.

Alvin Balent, M.D.
(Eye Surgeon)
Ft. Lauderdale, FL

After being involved in Olympic Sports as an athlete for over 20 years and after working directly with the health of Olympic and professional athletes, I have tried a great number of protein and food supplements. The greatest obstacle I find in working with good nutrition is that very often the athlete will consume large quantities of fat and refined carbohydrates to get the necessary nutrients for tissue building and repair. After becoming acquainted with Spirulina I began to see fewer allergic food reactions and faster recovery from workouts as well as injuries. I feel that Spirulina is a superior quality food because it contains small amounts of fat and large amounts of high quality protein and minerals. I recommend it for athletes as well as patients that want to go that extra mile to enhance their human performance potential.

Cordially,
James R. Wooley, D.C.
Irvine Health Center
Irvine, CA

Having had a background as a Naturopathic Physician, I find the formulation of Spirulina plankton to warrant it being called the food of the future. In fact, I wish it were available to everyone now, and I am doing my best to make it available in my practice.

I have personally used the [. . .]* program for about six months. I have always had to be a weight-watcher, and I am amazed that such a small amount can be so effective in controlling my appetite and weight, and in preventing feelings of hunger. I also find that it is excellent for the digestive and eliminative system and my general state of health which I have maintained during this period.

I do not hesitate to recommend Spirulina and its use by nutritional consultants in a dietary program.

> *Respectfully yours,*
> *s/s Ray Yancey, Ph.D.*
> *Executive Secretary*
> *International Academy*
> *of Nutritional Consultants*
> *Huntington Beach, CA*

P.S. As the Academy does not make endorsements, please construe this as my personal endorsement.

Editor's Introduction

Dr. Michael Sansone has been practicing chiropractic preventive health care for three years. He is currently director of the Irvine Health Center, a clinic with 2000 patients in Irvine, California. The Irvine Health Center's approach to helping the patient obtain optimum health is threefold: restoration of proper metabolism, normal spinal column/pelvis alignment, and balance of mind/brain functions. Dr. Sansone, whose background in nutrition includes 14 years of study, uses Spirulina as an essential part of this very thorough program with patients that range from Olympic athletes to arthritis victims.

In the following paper, Dr. Sansone describes the case histories of two of his patients, which he states would have been difficult or impossible to treat without a plankton such as Spirulina. In the first case, a 60-year old woman who suffered from fatigue, stiffness, memory loss, muscle aches, and depression was found to be malnourished because she could not properly digest her food. She *was* able to absorb Spirulina, however, and subsequently regained her metabolic balance, getting to the point where she could begin eating and digesting other foods again. Her health was restored.

The second patient, a ten-month old baby boy was unable to hold his head up, suffered chronic diarrhea, and showed retarded mental functioning. After beginning a diet of Spirulina the child improved immediately. Here again, malnutrition was a major problem, and Spirulina's easily digested proteins and rare carbohydrates made it the perfect diet for this severely weakened child.

Dr. Sansone concludes his paper with an excellent analysis of why Spirulina "works": how its unique plant cells can feed the cells of the human body with proteins and carbohydrates that are in "predigested" forms, instantly ready for use by our body.

THE USE OF SELECTED MICROBIOLOGICAL NUTRITION SUBSTANCE IN THE CLINICAL MANAGEMENT OF THE CHRONICALLY ILL.
by Michael Sansone, D.C.

Many failure cases can be successfully treated by supplementing the patient's diet with nutrients required in the healing response. The *Merck Manual* recognizes the physiological need for nutritional consideration in the management of chronic and acute disease states.[1] The recent announcement by the prestigious National Academy of Sciences linking the epitome of chronic, degenerative disease (cancer) to nutritional factors promises to usher in a new era of research, debate and interest in Clinical Nutrition.

One area that merits further research is the use of nutritional microbiological substances in the clinical management of the chronically ill. Japanese physicians and researchers have pioneered such work and report positive clinical results in cases of diabetes, hepatitis, chronic anemia, pancreatitis, cataracts, glaucoma and circular depilation.[2]

The author of this paper will present two case histories of patients that would be difficult or impossible to successfully treat without the use of microbiological nutrients. He will then discuss the biochemical and biophysical factors of the working hypotheses that attempt to describe the general mechanics involved in the positive clinical changes.

Case I.

A female, age 60, reported chronic fatigue, multiple joint pain and stiffness, vertigo, tinnitus, memory loss, muscular aches, vague chest pains and depression. She had been treated by physicians with muscle relaxant medication, valium and chelation therapy. She stated she felt much worse after the chelation therapy which had occurred a year before contacting my office.

Physical exam findings included blood pressure of 160/85 right sitting, 3/4-inch physiological short left, multiple vertebral fixations, negative Romberg, pulse 80, normal deep tendon reflexes of the upper and lower extremities. E.K.G. and cardiac stress testing results were normal.

Laboratory findings included elevated serum cholesterol, elevated triglycerides and an abnormal six-hour G.T.T. (dysinsulinism). Tissue mineral analysis results showed elevated lead, cadmium and calcium.

Radiographic exam of the chest was normal.

Chiropractic spinal adjustments produced a subjective improvement in joint mobility, subjective energy levels and vertigo. However, the chest pain, cerebral symptoms and tinnitis persisted. Provocative food testing and the Coco-pulse test indicated multiple food sensitivities. All routine food supplements tested produced microbiological food, Spirulina phytoplankton, to be taken in place of the stress producing diet. Four days of distilled water and a mono-diet of [. . .]* resulted in a dramatic reversal of the resisting symptoms. The patient was placed on a four-day rotational diet for six weeks and re-evaluated. Tolerable foods were reintroduced into the diet as indicated.

Follow-up evaluations after one year found the patient essentially asymptomatic and able to function at a high level of energy. The blood pressure stabilized at 125/84, serum cholesterol and triglycerides were normal. Elimination of toxic metals and restoration of calcium balance were objectified by post-treatment tissue mineral analysis.

DISCUSSION:

The patient was obviously subclinically malnourished and unable to digest the foods she depended upon for nutrients. By using a microbiological food, she was able to gradually gain enough strength to rotate her foods and eventually find an individual diet suitable for her maintenance program. Denatured vitamins/minerals had created severe biochemical imbalance.

Case II.

A male, age ten months, was carried into my office unable to hold his head up, with chronic diarrhea, retarded mental functioning and mottled teeth. The mother had followed orthodox pediatric therapy with no significant clinical improvement. The baby was repeatedly hospitalized for I.V. electrolyte replacement. Diagnosis was undetermined mental retardation with possible organic brain dysfunction. The patient was cytotoxically tested and found to be highly reactive to all foods tested as well as hydrocarbons.

Upper cervical, cranial and coccygeal adjustments produced modest (but encouraging) results in alertness and muscle strength but the dangerous loss of fluids and electrolytes due to the diarrhea was of great concern. The patient was placed on a mono-diet of Spirulina and immediate improvement was noted in bowel function, muscle strength, and alertness. The patient continued to improve and other foods were introduced into the diet gradually as his strength improved. Follow-up reports two years later show the child to be normal in all respects.

CASE DISCUSSION:

Again, we see a case of severe debilitation secondary to chronic malnutrition. Digestion requires energy and prudence would dictate that only compatible foods be introduced into the diet. Spirulina is easily digested and supplies protein in the form of biliproteins as well as carbohydrate in the form of rhamnose and glycogen. In essence, the algae predigests the food for us.

Biochemical/biophysical considerations of using Spirulina phytoplankton clinically

It would not be a hasty generalization to state that all cells are involved in the transmutation of matter into energy. Weak cells are, by definition, less effective in the bioenergy function than strong cells.

In the animal, cells form organs which form organ systems which form organisms. True health restoration begins at the cellular level. To improve the functioning of the cellular metabolism is to improve health in the organism.

Spirulina phytoplankton is a plant cell rich in animal metabolites. Unlike other plant cells, Spirulina has a cell wall that is readily digested by humans. The metabolites of the Spirulina cell are therefore readily available to human cells for assimilation into the energy producing mechanisms such as glycolysis and the Kreb's Citric Acid Cycle.

A glance at the analysis of Spirulina conducted by TNO, a UN-approved laboratory, reveals some interesting data. Spirulina contains all of the essential amino acids in a proportion compatible to human cellular requirements. Little energy is required to digest the amino acids as they are found to be "predigested" by the algae cell. The proteins found in Spirulina are biliproteins formed by the photosynthetic conjugation process. Humans who are manifesting dis-ease are found to be in an energy deficient state, and are often unable to digest their normal foods.

Spirulina is a very good source of porphyrin pigments both quantitatively and qualitatively. Porphyrin pigments play a vital role in animal cellular metabolism. They act as precursors to coenzymes by binding to minerals. Hemoglobin, Vitamin B-12 (cyanocobalamin), bilirubin and biliverdin are examples of substances containing porphyrin structures. Spirulina supplies biliproteins (in the form of phycocyanin) which react enzymatically with carbohydrates to form glycoproteins which are essential to cellular metabolism.

Spirulina also contains a unique form of carbohydrate that is also "predigested" for human assimilation; glycogen, found in animal cells, is also the storage form of sugar for the Spirulina algae. This form saves energy as the human cell can easily transmute glycogen into glucose without the excess utilization of energy. Additionally, the Spirulina phytoplankton contains the sugar rhamnose. Rhamnose is a metabolic by-product of rutinose, which is derived from rutin during animal metabolism. Thus the algae supplies a "predigested" carbohydrate ready for the energy-starved human cell to use.

The complete mechanism of cellular respiration is not completely understood. The Knowledge we do have is based upon concepts put forth in quantum mechanics. Energy liberated by the excited states of valence electrons is transferred within the cell. The cell itself is self-regulatory via D.N.A. inhibitory and facilitory, feedback mechanisms. It is logical to assume that by supplying the raw material, in an acceptable form, required for the efficient oxidation at the intracellular level one could expect an increase in cellular function. Spirulina appears to have a nonspecific effect by supplying precursors to vital cellular metabolites. In addition to the aforementioned amino acids, porphyrins and rhamnose, Spirulina phytoplankton also supplies carotenoids, minerals, steroids, lipids and numerous vitamins. It appears to be as complete a food as known by nutritional science.

The author has presented data that would hopefully stimulate other researchers to investigate the old/new idea of using a superior product of nature to supply the essential nutrients for humans. There is no doubt that nearly every human subsisting on "civilized" agribusiness foods is suffering from malnutrition of various degrees.[3, 4] The ability of the patient to respond to any form of therapy is directly proportional to the level of cellular functioning.

Cellular function is dependent upon the liberation of energy from the oxygen atom. The working hypothesis utilized by the author in the treatment of the chronically ill is based upon normalization of the cellular oxidation reaction through the use of individualized nutritional therapy. Other researchers have established metabolic individuality.[5, 6, 7] Future research into individualized typing and the use of microbiological nutritional substances such as Spirulina phytoplankton promises to yield data correlative with the author's empirical and clinical experience.

REFERENCES

1. *MERCK MANUAL*, Pg. 1147.

2. *THE SECRETS OF SPIRULINA. MEDICAL DISCOVERIES OF JAPANESE DOCTORS.* Edited by Christopher Hills. University of the Trees Press. Boulder Creek, CA.

3. *HUMAN NUTRITION, Report No. 2.* Science and Education Staff. USDA 1973.

4. *DIET AND KILLER DISEASES WITH PRESS REACTION AND ADDITIONAL INFORMATION.* Prepared by Select Committee on Nutrition and Human Needs, U.S. Senate, Jan. 1977.

5. Williams, Roger. *BIOCHEMICAL INDIVIDUALITY.*

6. Watson, George. *NUTRITION AND YOUR MIND.* Harper and Row, 1972.

7. Rahe, Fred. *METABOLIC ECOLOGY.* Wedgestone Press, 1982.

I would like to say the following about Spirulina:

There are several uses for which I recommend Spirulina.

I have found [. . .]* increases energy in some cases, especially in those deficient in protein, not an uncommon problem in our junkaholic society today.

In cases where there is a deficiency of trace minerals such as chromium or potassium and a blood sugar problem, [. . .]* is helpful in restoring the natural balance, especially when complemented with the product msx*.

As an appetite suppressor, [. . .]* is effective in many cases, when the tablets are taken before the meal. Hunger is, of course, a complex thing, so while [. . .]* suppresses pure hunger itself, it doesn't always work with the overweight due to psychological over-riding -- in other words there are often many causes for overeating in addition to simple physical hunger.

I have found [. . .]* good for tired adrenals, not as an end in itself but to help the patient get over the rough spots while solving the stress problem.

[. . .]* is an ideal product for the vegetarian because of the high quality of its protein and because of its high content of Vitamin B-12 which alleviates the anemia often found in these patients. It is, of course, a food they can eat to obtain these needed nutrients without going against their religion.

Stevan Cordas, D.O., F.A.P.M.,
Past President, International
Academy of Preventative Medicine
Medford, TX

I have been using for my family, self and professionally, Spirulina for the past two years. The results have been most satisfactory. Individuals who thought they could never lose weight are very happily wearing 2 to 5 sizes smaller in their clothing. One individual, a nurse, lost 90 pounds over a one year period.

It is my pleasure to most heartily recommend Spirulina Plankton. Naturally, with metabolism differing, there will be a 1 to 2% non-response, or perhaps an individual just not following the simple directions, e.g. not drinking a full 8 oz. glass of water with the plankton.

To conclude, after 20 years of practice, I have not found any substance that would give the drastic amount of satisfaction that is found with Spirulina.

> *Sincerely,*
> *Marquetta (Myk) Hungerford,*
> *Ph.D., R.M.T.*
> *National Education Director*
> *American Massage & Therapy*
> *Association, Inc.*
> *Costa Mesa, CA*

In response to your request for my experience in the use of Spirulina I can tell you that I have used it personally as well as with selective patients in my practice.

In my experience it has been helpful in certain cases of hypoglycemia, with diabetic patients in better maintaining their diet and preventing weight gain, and also in patients with exogenous obesity as part of their dietary regimen. It is helpful in young people who need between meals or after school snacks. As you know it is high in protein and low in carbohydrates. One 500 mg. tablet only contains two calories.

As you also know Spirulina is an excellent food substitute containing approximately 71% quality protein. The exact percentage varies with growth conditions. It contains all eight amino acids, vitamins, organically bound minerals and even provides some of the essential fatty acids.

> *Sincerely,*
> *Gasper F. Ruffino, D.O.*
> *Livonia, MI*

152

REFERENCES

Beasley, Sonia. *The Spirulina Cookbook*. Boulder Creek, California: University of the Trees Press, 1982.

Challem, Jack Joseph. *Spirulina: What it is . . . the Health Benefits It Can Give You*. New Canaan, Connecticut: Keats Publishing, Inc., 1981.

Hills, Christopher. *Imprisoned Light*. Boulder Creek, California: Journal of Nutritional Microbiology, 1980.

Hills, Christopher. *The Joy of Slimming*. Boulder Creek, California: Microalgae International Sales Corporation, 1982.

Hills, Christopher. *Rejuvenating the Body through Fasting with Spirulina Plankton*. Boulder Creek, California: University of the Trees Press, 1979.

Hills, Christopher, ed. *The Secrets of Spirulina: Medical Discoveries of Japanese Doctors*. Boulder Creek, California: University of the Trees Press, 1980.

Hills, Christopher and Nakamura, Hiroshi. *Food From Sunlight*. Boulder Creek, California: University of the Trees Press, 1978.

Nakamura, Hiroshi. *Spirulina: Food for a Hungry World*. Boulder Creek, California: University of the Trees Press, 1982.

Switzer, Larry. *Spirulina: The Whole Food Revolution*. New York, New York: Bantam Books, 1982.